LAY SAINTS
Models of Family Life

LAY SAINTS
Models of Family Life

JOAN CARROLL CRUZ

TAN Books
Charlotte, North Carolina

Cover design by David Ferris.
www.davidferrisdesign.com

Cover image: *The Holy Family*.

Cataloging-in-Publication data on file with the Library of Congress.

ISBN: 978-0-89555-722-3

Printed and bound in India

TAN Books
Charlotte, North Carolina
www.TANBooks.com
2015

This book is
dedicated with love
to
The Holy Family

CONTENTS

YOUTH

CONTENTS

INTRODUCTION

A NATIONAL Catholic magazine polled a thousand of its readers to learn what they believe about the saints. The magazine reported that while news reports on the nation's Catholics have highlighted disagreements with traditional Church teachings, sixty-seven percent of the survey's respondents said they prayed to the saints as much, or more, than they did years ago. Sixty-eight percent of the respondents said they tried to imitate the lives of the saints.

Mentioned as the four favorite saints were the Blessed Mother, St. Joseph, St. Francis of Assisi and St. Thérèse of Lisieux (the Little Flower). With the exception of the Blessed Mother and St. Joseph, who are in a unique category, we are left with a Franciscan brother and a Discalced Carmelite cloistered nun. While we can admire the virtues of St. Francis and St. Thérèse, the lifestyles of these two saints, and other saints of religious orders, are far removed, to say the least, from those of lay people.

Although the exact number of canonized saints is unknown, we know, of course, that the greater majority have been members of religious orders. We love them, we admire them, we wish to imitate them. But how can a mother with small children, a wife with a difficult husband, a young bride with in-law problems—how can they really relate to the nun who lived in the quiet of a cloister, the nun who lived in a community where everyone shared the work of the house? How can they relate to the saints of religious orders whose lives were arranged in an orderly manner and who had designated times for quiet prayer and who had little or no financial problems?

One might wonder whether these saints of the cloister would have merited their titles if they had remained in the world to face the conflicts and dangers confronted by ordinary lay people.

It is profitable, of course, for lay people to love these saints, to pray to them and to imitate their virtues as much as they are able. But it seems that lay people would draw more encouragement to advance in prayer and virtue and would derive more consolation in their trials by examining the troubles and temptations of those saints who lived and died as lay members of the Church.

St. Teresa of Ávila suggests that "we need to cultivate and think upon, and seek the companionship of those saints who, though living on earth like ourselves, have accomplished such great deeds for God." In these four volumes, then, are the lives of lay saints who have, so to speak, "lived on earth like ourselves." Represented here are single men and women, mothers and fathers, soldiers and servants, doctors and lawyers, the humble and the noble—all who have met the difficulties and challenges of the secular life and triumphed over them.

Their virtues are to be admired, but most of all imitated. May we benefit from their example and from their prayers.

—Joan Carroll Cruz

PREFACE
A WORD ABOUT THE
BLESSED VIRGIN MARY

A BOOK about lay saints would be incomplete without mentioning the preeminent model for lay people, the Blessed Mother. But what could be said here that has not been mentioned about her already in numerous biographies and devotional works? We have only to delve into these to find a solicitous and understanding mother, a kindly and generous friend, a consoling companion, and a ready and willing intercessor with God.

Although it is known that Mary was free from sin, full of grace, blessed among women and the fairest honor of our race, yet she was not exempt from countless trials and hardships. She, who was the model of saints throughout the ages, should be the particular ideal of lay people, since Mary was an exemplary member of our lay ranks. She was, of course, a young bride, a young mother, a housekeeper, and a widow. . . .

May this Immaculate Mother pray for us, that in our imitation of the saints, we can advance in virtue and eventually join her and her sainted children in our heavenly homeland.

LAY SAINTS
Models of Family Life

But if it seem evil to you to serve the Lord, you have your choice: choose this day that which pleaseth you, whom you would rather serve, whether the gods which your fathers served in Mesopotamia, or the gods of the Amorrhites, in whose land you dwell: but as for me and my house we will serve the Lord.

—Joshua 24:15

HUSBANDS, WIVES, AND PARENTS

ONE

SAINT ADALBALD
OF OSTREVANT

D. 650

AS THE son of a distinguished family, Adalbald spent much of his time in the court of Dagobert I and Clovis II and may have been the Duke of Douai. An ideal Christian noble, he was a general favorite among the courtiers.

While on an expedition in Gascony, Adalbald became friends with a noble lord named Ernald, whose daughter, Rictrude, became Adalbald's bride. The wedding was performed with great pomp, but the union did not please certain members of the bride's family. Yet, in spite of a critical assessment of the groom by his in-laws and their dire predictions for the couple's future, the marriage proved to be a happy one. Early in their wedded life, the young couple became interested in performing works of mercy and spent time visiting the sick, relieving the poor, feeding the hungry, and converting prisoners.

Four children were born to them: a son, Mauront, and three daughters, Eusebia, Clotsind, and Adalsind. All four children imitated their parents in the ways of virtue and acts of charity.

In the year 650, sixteen years after his marriage, Adalbald

was recalled to Gascony, never to return. When he reached the vicinity of Perigueux, he was attacked and killed by a number of his wife's vindictive relatives.

When news of her husband's death reached Rictrude, she was overcome with grief. Even so, she managed to obtain possession of her husband's body, which was buried with honor.

Following Adalbald's death and after her children were grown, Rictrude entered the double monastery for men and women at Marchiennes, which she had previously founded. This monastery was so arranged that the living accommodations and prayer areas were entirely separate. Only the chapel was shared, but even this was divided into sections. Accompanying Rictrude into the monastery were her two younger daughters, Adalsind and Clotsind, as well as her only son, Mauront, who left the world and the Frankish court to receive the tonsure in his mother's presence.

Following Rictrude's death, Clotsind succeeded her mother as abbess of the monastery. The third daughter, Eusebia, entered the monastery of Haimage, which had been founded by her great-grandmother, St. Gertrude of Haimage.

The remains of St. Adalbald rested in the Monastery of St. Amandles-Eaux in Elanone (Elnon), France, but afterward his head was taken to Douai. This we learn from an ancient manuscript of the Church of St. Ame, where there was, at one time, a magnificent chapel dedicated to Sts. Adalbald, Rictrude and their son, St. Mauront. Exhibited there for public veneration were statues of the holy trio. That of St. Adalbald was draped in a robe covered with lilies; St. Rictrude's statue was clothed in a Benedictine habit and held a miniature replica of the Abbey of Marchiennes in her hand;

and St. Mauront was represented with a sceptre in his right hand and towers in his left.

The whole family—father, mother, three daughers and one son—are honored as saints of the Church. Also included in this holy gathering are Adalbald's grandmother, St. Gertrude of Haimage, and Rictrude's sister, St. Bertha, who after being widowed became a nun and the foundress of the Monastery of Blangy in Artois.

TWO

SAINT ADELAIDE

D. 999

THE history of St. Adelaide (Adelheid) is dominated by the tenth-century power struggle and intrigue of certain parties for control of the Kingdom of Italy. Adelaide was born into this struggle, being the daughter of Rudolph II, King of Burgundy, who was at war with Hugh of Provence for the Italian crown. In 933, the rivals reached a peace agreement which stipulated that Adelaide, the daughter of one rival, should marry Lothaire, the son of the other rival. Adelaide was then only two years old. Fourteen years later her brother, Conrad of Burgundy, arranged the marriage and thereby fulfilled the contract. This marriage produced one child, a daughter, who was named Emma.

As a result of this marriage, Adelaide's husband, Lothaire, was considered the King of Italy. However, Berengarius, the Marquis of Ivrea, came upon the scene and claimed the Kingdom of Italy for himself. When Lothaire suddenly died in 950, it was suspected that he had been poisoned by Berengarius, who succeeded him. Berengarius then attempted to force the widow Adelaide to marry his son, Adalbert. When she refused, Berengarius treated her with brutality and kept her in almost solitary confinement in the Castle of Garda.

From there she was rescued by a priest named Martin, who is said to have dug a subterranean passage by which she escaped. Adelaide remained concealed in the woods until her friend Alberto Uzzo, the Duke of Canossa, heard of the rescue and conveyed her to his castle.

While this was taking place, the Italian nobles, having grown weary of Berengarius, invited Otto the Great of Germany to invade and seize the country for himself. Otto met little resistance and promptly defeated Berengarius. To consolidate his authority in Italy, Otto married Adelaide at Pavia in the year 951. Adelaide had been a widow for one year and was twenty years younger than Otto. Of Adelaide's second marriage, five children were born: Otto II, Henry, Bruno, and two daughters, who eventually became nuns.

Otto, it seems, had been married earlier to the daughter of Athelstan of England. Otto's son by this marriage, Rudolph, was jealous of the influence of his stepmother and her children and became a source of friction and rebellion. In spite of this, the German people accepted the gentle Adelaide and held her in the highest regard.

Berengarius once again instigated trouble in Italy, and when he finally invaded the Papal States, Pope John XII appealed to Otto for help. When Otto took his forces across the Alps, Berengarius retreated. In 962 Otto was crowned emperor at Rome. Little is related about Adelaide for the following ten years, until the death of Otto the Great in 973 and the succession of her son Otto II.

During the reign of her son, trouble once again brought Adelaide to prominence. Although Otto II had many worthy traits, he permitted his wife, Theophania, and other counselors to turn him against his mother. Some suspect that the daughter-in-law resented Adelaide because of the saint's liberality to the poor. Because of the unpleasant atmosphere at court, Adelaide left and went to her brother, Conrad, at Vienna. She appealed to St. Majolus, Abbot of Cluny, to effect a reconciliation. This was eventually brought about at Pavia, with her son asking pardon on his knees for his unkindness.

Trouble once more shadowed Adelaide when Otto II died and left as his successor his son, Otto III, who was then an infant. The child's mother, Theophania, assumed the duties of regent. With her troublesome daughter-in-law in complete control and as yet unreconciled, Adelaide again left the court. When Theophania died suddenly in 991, Adelaide was recalled to serve as regent in her place.

Adelaide's administration was dependent upon the wise guidance of Adalbert of Magdeburg, St. Majolus, and St. Odilo of Cluny, who wrote about the saintly regent. These holy men reported that Adelaide was forgiving to her enemies and proved herself generous in her dealings. She founded and restored monasteries of monks and nuns, maintained a peaceful religious atmosphere at court, and was zealous in her attempts to convert the pagans of the northern and eastern frontiers.

When she was sixty-eight years of age, St. Adelaide died while on a journey to Burgundy to reconcile Rudolph III with his subjects. It was December 16, 999.

Although St. Adelaide is not mentioned in the *Roman Martyrology,* she is greatly revered in Germany, where her name appears on their calendars.

THREE

BLESSED ALBERT
OF BERGAMO

D. 1279

BLESSED Albert's virtuous parents were peasant farmers in the little town of Villa d'Ogna, near Bergamo, Italy. Albert began his prayerful life at an early age, being only seven when he began to practice penance and perform works of charity. At about the same time, he also began his laborious work in the fields. While performing his chores, he kept himself in continual recollection and made use of the sights and sounds of nature to raise his mind and heart to God.

When Albert came of age, his father suggested that he marry. In obedience to his father's wishes he married a young peasant girl, with whom he lived for many years in perfect harmony. After a time Albert's wife, who remained childless, began to imitate him in his pious exercises.

However, upon the death of her father-in-law, Albert's wife underwent a sudden change of disposition and from then on became a continual trial to her husband. She bitterly reproached and criticized him for spending time in prayer and for his generosity to the poor. Bl. Albert is said to have possessed an unalterable sweetness and to have been patient and silent while enduring his domestic difficulties. After some time his wife died, leaving him a widower.

Sometime after Albert was widowed, a group of powerful nobles seized his property. He left the neighborhood and settled at Cremona, where he again worked as a farmer, earning for himself the title of "the diligent laborer." There he performed various miracles, and gave to the poor all that he could spare from his meager wages.

Albert placed himself under the direction of the Dominican Fathers whose monastery was near his lodging and was accepted into the Dominican Third Order. From then on he devoted himself to the care of the sick and poor, visiting them and performing useful services to relieve their distress. He also kept a prayerful vigil during their final agony and saw to their burial.

After occupying himself in this manner for many years, Albert felt himself called to undertake the life of a pilgrim. He is known to have traveled to the Holy Land at least once, to have visited the sanctuaries and shrines of Spain, and to have journeyed to Rome on nine occasions. He remained recollected during his travels, and as Proctor relates, he "beguiled the monotony of the way by singing hymns or reciting psalms."

After traveling for several years, Albert settled once more in Cremona and resumed his work among the distressed, welcoming into his poor home those in extreme poverty and travelers who needed rest and lodging.

When Albert was about seventy years old, he became ill and asked for Last Rights. When the priest delayed in coming, it is said that the Holy Eucharist was brought to him by a white dove, which then disappeared.

Bl. Albert died on May 7, 1279. Those who were preparing a grave for him in the cemetery found it impossible to penetrate the ground with their tools. For this reason it became necessary to return the remains to the church. There, on the very spot where he had so often prayed, was found a vault which had been mysteriously prepared to accept his body. The poor who had so often benefitted from his generosity attended the funeral service, which was conducted by the Bishop with the assistance of the Dominican Fathers.

The veneration for Bl. Albert which soon developed was approved by Pope Benedict XIV, who also gave permission for a Mass and Office to be celebrated in Albert's honor by members of the Dominican Order and by the clergy of the Dioceses of Bergamo and Cremona.

FOUR

BLESSED ANGELA
OF FOLIGNO

C. 1248–1309

ANGELA was born in the city of Foligno, Italy, where she derived all the benefits of being reared as a member of a prominent family. She was married to a man of substantial means and became the mother of several children. In her early life she was careless and worldly, and according to her own account, her life was not only pleasure-seeking and self-indulgent, but was also sinful. One source tells that, "Forgetful of her dignity and duties as wife and mother, she fell into sin and led a disorderly life."

Quite suddenly Angela experienced a complete transformation—a sudden, vivid conversion in which the life she had thought harmless, she now saw in its true perspective as sinful. As a result of this, she earnestly wanted to make reparation by doing penance and performing works of mercy. She took as her model St. Francis of Assisi, and became a tertiary in the Franciscan Third Order.

As a tertiary she continued her normal life in the world, but now spent more time in prayer and penance—more than that which was prescribed by the Rule. Then, her life became one of great sorrow when death claimed her husband and her

15

mother. Finally, one by one, all her children died. Brother Arnold, a Friar Minor, who was her confessor, tells how cruelly she suffered as blow after blow fell upon her. Her conversion had been so complete, however, that despite her great sorrow, she accepted her trial with complete resignation to the will of God.

Soon after these losses, Angela began to experience visions. In one of these she was reminded that if she meant to be perfect, she must sell all that she had and follow St. Francis in his absolute poverty. As a result of this vision, she sold a castle that was very dear to her.

Although Angela experienced many visions and ecstasies, Brother Arnold wrote that she was ever humble, so that the greater the ecstasy, the deeper was her humility. The details of her mystical experiences were dictated to Brother Arnold, who recorded them in a book entitled *(Book of) Visions and Instructions,* which contains seventy chapters.

We are also told that Bl. Angela experienced the mystical marriage with Our Lord and bore on her body the wounds of the stigmata. Although Angela always remained a lay person, a number of her fellow tertiaries—both men and women—looked to her for guidance. These also received her dying prayer as they stood around her deathbed.

Bl. Angela died on January 4, 1309. Her remains are found in the Church of St. Francis at Foligno, where the many miracles worked at her tomb prompted Pope Innocent XII to sanction the veneration paid to her. Bl. Angela of Foligno is considered one of the Church's great mystics.

FIVE

BLESSED ANNA
MARIA TAIGI

1769–1837

THE life story of this beata is distinguished by serious family trials, painful physical ailments, an intense spiritual life, and extraordinary mystical gifts.

Her father was Louis Giannetti, a pharmacist who kept a shop in Siena; her mother, Mary Santa Masil, was a good Catholic of lowly fortune. Anna Maria was born on May 29, 1769, and was baptized the same day in the Church of St. John the Baptist at Siena. Her early childhood was happily spent in the city made famous 400 years earlier by St. Catherine.

But when Anna Maria was six years old, her father's business failed. She and her impoverished parents moved to Rome, where they found a home in the crowded *dei Monti* quarter. In this area there also lived St. Benedict Joseph Labre, whom Anna Maria and her parents undoubtedly saw on many occasions. When St. Benedict Labre died, the future beata was among the many children who ran through the streets crying, "The Saint is dead! The Saint is dead!" Anna Maria's mother prepared the saint's body for burial, since she was accustomed to performing such acts of charity.

While Anna Maria's parents worked as domestics, she attended the free school which had been founded by St. Lucia Filippini. In this school her education included lessons in cooking and sewing, occupations that would greatly benefit her in later life. She learned to read, but she never learned to write. Her formal schooling ended abruptly when she contracted smallpox, which left its traces on her face. After recovering from the disease, she remained at home to perform the household chores, which greatly relieved her working mother.

Anna Maria is known to have received the Sacrament of Penance at the age of seven. At eleven she was confirmed in the Basilica of St. John Lateran, and at thirteen she made her First Holy Communion in the parish church of St. Francis of Paola. Although the family performed many pious practices, which included reciting their prayers together both morning and night and often saying the Rosary, their household was not particularly happy. Neither father nor mother ever adjusted to the failure of their business and the harsh life they were forced to endure as a result. The mother, it seems, found her lot particularly hard to bear, while Anna's father "vented his ill humor on the child, ill-treating her without reason."

Anna Maria's childhood did not last long. At the age of thirteen she was employed in a shop run by two elderly ladies. Engaged in winding silk and cutting out dresses, she returned home in the evenings only to take up other chores, which included washing the clothes, cooking the meals, and cleaning the house.

In 1787 Anna Maria joined both her parents at the Maccarani palace, where all three were employed as servants.

The burdens of poverty were eased considerably for the little family, and it was here that the attractive child matured into a great beauty. Her mistress, Maria Serra, joined Anna Maria's mother in frequently praising the girl's charms—until eventually Anna Maria was spending more and more time before her mirror. According to the Decree of Beatification, "The beautiful young girl early encountered the dangers that imperil chastity." Her first biographer, Msgr. Luquet, a friend of the family, states only that there was an "occasion" which made Anna Maria realize certain dangers and made her resolve to "shelter her virtue by giving it the safeguard of a chaste marriage."

After three years spent in the service of Madame Serra, Anna Maria met her future husband. He was not a man of wealth, as her mother had hoped, but was a lowly porter by the name of Domenico Taigi, who served at the palace of Prince Chigi. He was a handsome young man of medium height and healthy constitution—but, according to the Decree of Beatification, "His manners were rough and uncultured and his temperament unamiable." He nevertheless won the heart of twenty-year-old Anna Maria. The marriage was solemnized six weeks later on January 7, 1790 by the parish priest of St. Marcel in the Corso. Many years later, after Anna Maria's death, her daughter Sophia testified for the Process:

> My mother told me that if she arranged everything within forty days, it was because she did not want to be forever at home "warming the seat," but to get on with it once she was assured of a good and honorable future; delay could only bring boredom and danger. She never regretted her action. My father was a rough character, and anyone but my mother

would certainly have repented of marrying such a man; but although he tried her patience sorely, she was always glad that she had married him.

During the first year of her marriage, Anna Maria succumbed to a bit of human weakness. To please her husband she engaged in a measure of vanity and took to wearing jewelry and pretty clothes. Nevertheless, she was always modest and was always a credit and joy to her proud husband. After these early years she met Fr. Angelo Verandi, a Servite priest who was to lead her from the vanities of the world to a life of sanctity. Although many charges have been justly levelled at Domenico, he seems to have been moved by grace at the time of Anna Maria's call to a life of self-sacrifice and virtue. In his deposition, Domenico, himself, stated what took place at that time:

> The Servant of God, while yet in the flower of her youth, gave up, for the love of God, all the jewelry she used to wear—rings, earrings, necklaces and so on, and took to wearing the plainest possible clothes. She asked my permission for this, and I gave it to her with all my heart, for I saw she was entirely given to the love of God.

At the age of twenty-one, when Anna Maria was the mother of a new baby, she received Domenico's permission to be received as a tertiary in the Trinitarian Order. During the first year of this profession she was granted an extraordinary favor that was to endure for forty-seven years. This privilege took the form of a constant vision of a luminous disc, somewhat like a miniature sun, that maintained a position above and before her. Atop the upper rays was a large crown of interwoven thorns, with two lengthy thorns on either side curving downward so that they crossed each other under the solar disc, their points emerging on either side of the rays. In the center sat a beautiful woman with her face raised toward heaven. In this vision Anna Maria saw things of the natural, moral, and divine order and could see present or future events anywhere in the world, as well as the state of grace of living individuals and the fate of the departed. The Decree of Beatification speaks of it as "a prodigy unique in the annals of sanctity." In this sun she also received answers to difficult theological questions and observed scenes of the life of Christ.

In addition to this perpetual vision, Anna Maria was blessed with frequent ecstasies, and was able to read hearts, work miracles of healing, and predict future events. She was also blessed with various visions and occasionally was visited by St. Joseph, to whom she was particularly devoted. He appeared not as an old man, but as a strong, handsome young man, a little older than the Blessed Mother.

Although favored with these spiritual privileges, Anna Maria nevertheless remained a diligent housewife and a mother who in twelve years bore seven children, three of whom died in infancy. Another preceded his mother in death. We are told that Anna Maria herself placed her children in their shrouds.

Domenico tells how Anna Maria was faithful both to the practice of virtue and the duties of her vocation:

> I can assert in very truth that from the beginning of our marriage she never refused my rights, but never asserted her own. She contracted no debts, because she always guided her outlay by her income. If any of us fell ill she lavished every attention on us, to the extent of omitting, when necessary,

her Mass and her devotions. As for me, I have always thought in the past and say now that God took this excellent servant from me because I was not worthy to have her.

Considering Domenico's many faults and the trials inflicted on Anna Maria by her parents, who lived with the Taigi family, one can say that the beata's life was one lengthy martyrdom and an exercise of continual virtue. For a description of Domenico's faults and shortcomings we have the words of his daughter Sophie:

> My father was as pious and earnest a man as one could desire, but of such a fiery, exacting, haughty and wild temperament as to amaze one. On coming home he would whistle or knock, and we had immediately to dash to open the door at the risk of breaking our necks. In fact, twice my sister Mariuccia fell down through rushing too quickly to meet him, and on one of these occasions she had one of my baby daughters in her arms.
>
> If everything was not just as he wanted it he came in furious, and would go so far as to snatch hold of the tablecloth, where the dinner was served, and throw everything to the four winds. Everything had to be prepared to the tick, the soup hot in the tureen, the chair in place. He was as exacting in the matter of his clothes and of everything else.

To gain the children's obedience, Domenico frequently resorted to using a stick. One day, in order to avoid a beating, one of the children ran from the house. In a rage, Domenico tossed an armchair through a window. He was also given to using foul language in front of the children, but in the end Anna Maria succeeded in curing him of that habit through her patience and gentleness.

In addition to his exacting nature, fits of anger, impatience and coarse manners, Domenico was also jealous and protective of his wife. Domenico himself stated, "If I saw anyone annoying her I saw to it that it cost him dearly." An example of this was the time when Anna Maria, who was then pregnant, was going to church in the company of her husband. It was a great feastday with many people attending. A soldier, whose duty it was to keep order, nudged Anna Maria into place. Domenico's temper was immediately aroused. He attacked the soldier, verbally abused him, took away his carbine and began to beat him. Witnesses succeeded in separating the two before the soldier was seriously injured.

Domenico's temper was likewise provoked by women whose wagging tongues spoke ill of his wife. He relates that:

> Although she was at pains to do good to all and sundry, there were people with whispering tongues who gave her no rest, whether it was because they were jealous at seeing so many persons of distinction at our house, or because the devil induced them to beset her. But I could not be with her everywhere. Moreover, I saw that the Servant of God was pained when I took a hand in these matters, so in the end I said to her: "Do what you like and as you like; if you wish people to throw stones at you and to suffer thus at their hands, you are free to do so."

But there were times when Domenico could not restrain himself against those who spoke against his wife. Once when he heard that someone had referred to his wife by saying, "That sorceress has just passed," he:

> made a violent complaint to the woman's husband, and told him that if he did not succeed in making his wife control her tongue he would cut it out. The scatter-tongue, on coming home, was so beaten by her husband that she had to stay in bed for several days . . . Finally she [Anna Maria] paid a visit

to the woman, brought her some delicacies, prayed for her cure and obtained it.

Domenico also told of a woman who "had the hardihood to calumniate my wife's honor. I had the wretch put in prison, but my wife was grieved about it and did all she could to obtain her release."

In spite of all her husband's faults, Anna Maria was devoted to him—and there were times of gentleness and peace. Domenico again praises his wife:

> I wish to say this, for the glory of God, that I lived for forty-eight years or so with this saintly soul and never did I hear from her a word of impatience or discord. We lived in a perpetual peace as of Paradise. I used to go home often dead tired and a little distraught after my day's work and difficulties with my employers, and she would restore my serenity of mind.

Besides being ever alert to her husband's changing moods, the beata had in her household other difficult personalities— her own parents. With Domenico always on the verge of resorting to anger, Anna Maria's irritable mother apparently found pleasure in provoking him. Anna Maria is said to have gone from one to the other recommending patience. Anna Maria's mother became even more difficult as she grew older. She was frequently impatient, but nevertheless, Anna Maria did all she could for her and watched over her night and day when she became ill. When she died at the age of seventy-three, her last moments were spent in the arms of her devoted daughter.

Louis Giannetti, Anna Maria's father, was likewise difficult. After Madame Serra died, Louis lost his position as servant and squandered his small pension roaming Italy.

When this was gone he lived at his daughter's expense, while refusing to enter her home. Anna Maria found lodging for him and a position as a porter at an orphanage. When poor health made it impossible for her father to work, Anna Maria somehow found ways to satisfy his needs. He seems to have been disagreeable and to have made a practice of complaining. Frequently in a bad temper, he was often found sitting on the stairs of his daughter's home. Since he refused to enter the house, Anna Maria joined him on the stairs to wash him, comb his hair, mend his clothes and feed him.

"My father-in-law was smitten with a horrible leprosy," Domenico wrote, but with all the care Anna Maria gave him in cleansing the repulsive sores and performing the other services for him, he was never known to have thanked her. She prepared her father for death and obtained the Last Sacraments for him. Domenico observed, "One would think that God gave the Servant of God such parents simply to put her great virtue to a keener test."

Because of Anna Maria's infused knowledge and high degree of sanctity, she was frequently consulted by distinguished persons, including Pope Leo XII, Pope Gregory XVI, Napoleon's mother, Cardinal Fesch and Sts. Vincent Pallotti, Gaspar del Bufalo and Mary Euphrasia Pelletier. Many, too, were the simple folk who wanted advice from her on temporal and spiritual matters or who wanted to ask for Anna Maria's prayers for a cure or a favor. But Anna Maria always knew where her first duties lay. Domenico noted:

> Sometimes, on coming home to change my clothes, I found the house full of people. Instantly my wife left everybody, lords and prelates, and hurried to receive me, to brush me

down and to wait on me, with the greatest charm for me and the greatest satisfaction to herself. You could see that what she did, she did with all her heart—down to settling my shoe laces.

Throughout Anna Maria's life, difficulties seem to have constantly increased in number. When her son Camillo married, he brought his bride to live with him in his parents' already-crowded home, staying for two years. As if this were not enough, it is said that the daughter-in-law "was a difficult character, because she wanted to be the mistress." With her usual tact and charity, Anna Maria was successful in reminding the young bride of her proper position in the household.

Somehow Anna Maria maintained a schedule of prayer in spite of the clash of personalities, the overcrowded house, her many household responsibilities, and the almost steady stream of visitors to her home. There were family prayers in the morning; after supper there was the recitation of the Rosary, the reading from the life of the saint of the day, and the singing of hymns. On Sundays the whole family attended Holy Mass, then the girls went with their mother to the hospital to perform acts of charity.

Anna Maria was also careful that her children received instructions in their faith and that they behaved properly. When it was necessary, her children were dutifully reprimanded. Her daughter Sophie related that "Mamma loved us all tenderly and with an equal love that had no favorites. She used the stick, if necessary, but in moderation, and preferred to make us go without our dinner or to put us on dry bread."

Anna Maria also taught her children the value of keeping busy. Sophie reported, "She herself was never idle a minute;

she was always at work. She used to say: 'Laziness is the mother of all the vices.'" If Anna Maria taught the value of industry, she likewise gave a good example in this regard and maintained a busy needle. She made her husband's trousers and coats, and when he was unemployed she supported the family by making bodices, petticoats, half-boots, and socks. She regularly worked from two to three hours after midnight; then, after only two hours sleep, she was up for early Mass and Communion. We are told that when illness forced her to stay in bed she set herself to mending linen, and never remained idle.

When the children were older, there were other problems. For a brief time Anna Maria's son Alessandro was imprisoned, which caused the beata great heartache. Later, when he married, he and his wife—who came from a poor family—found great difficulty in meeting their financial obligations. Anna Maria gently recommended employment for her daughter-in-law who, having little, nevertheless wanted to be maintained in a gentle lifestyle. In the end, the beata taught both her daughters-in-law how to be thrifty and useful.

Anna Maria's younger daughter, Mariuccia, never married; and although in her youth she was reportedly vain and lazy, she died with a reputation for holiness, having survived her mother by forty-eight years.

Sophie was her mother's joy. She married well and became the mother of six children. When Sophie was widowed, Anna Maria welcomed her and her children into her household. Sophie died thirty years after her mother and was buried at her side in the Church of St. Chrysogonus.

To the troubles inflicted on Anna Maria by members

of her family and the burden of her impoverished state, she added penances and mortifications. We are told that "She was self-denying, especially on Fridays," but she likewise fasted on Saturdays and on Wednesdays in honor of St. Joseph. Her portion of food was always meager, and she was inclined to an almost continual thirst, which she refused to satisfy completely. Domenico observed that she never drank water between meals, even in the heat of summertime, and that at dinner she drank only a few sips at a time so as to mortify her thirst. Additionally, Anna Maria wore articles of penance and suffered from several physical maladies including asthma, almost continual headaches, chronic rheumatic troubles, a hernia, and pains in the ears so fierce that the beata frequently wrapped a band around her head. She also had sharp pains in her eyes, which were particularly sensitive to light. Eventually she lost the sight of one eye, and in her last years she was all but blind in the other.

We learn of the beata's interior life from Cardinal Pedicini, as well as from Msgr. Natali and from her director of thirty years, Father Philip-Louis of St. Nicholas, a Discalced Carmelite. In addition to the sustaining vision of the miraculous sun, we are told that frequently, while she was engaged in simple household chores, Anna Maria would be seized by an ecstasy or a vision of Our Lord, and she was known to have occasionally levitated. She recognized souls in a state of grace by the sweet fragrance of their souls, and upon entering a church she knew immediately at which altar the Blessed Sacrament was reserved. She is known to have cured many by virtue of a prayer and the Sign of the Cross.

Often, at the moment of Communion, Anna Maria saw

the Host come to life. Once she saw Jesus in the form of a child lying upon the petals of a white lily. He spoke softly to her: "I am the flower of the fields and the lily of the valley. In this crowd of people that you see in the church there are scarcely two souls truly sincere in their love. The others are equally ready to come to church or to go to the theater."

Frequently demons assaulted Anna Maria in ways that are reminiscent of those attacks experienced by the Curé of Ars. They often appeared in horrible forms and frequently disturbed her prayers by suggesting unclean imaginings and doubts against the Faith. The remedy used by the beata against the devils was the same as that recommended by St. Teresa of Avila—holy water.

Anna Maria's married life lasted forty-eight years. At the age of sixty-eight, on October 26, 1836, the beata took to her bed, never to leave it. For seven months she suffered an increase in her bodily ailments, yet we are told that she preserved a miraculous peace that never left her. After a vision of Our Lord, and after delivering a message to each of her children, she thanked Domenico for the care he had taken of her. Supported by the prayers of those around her and by a last absolution, Anna Maria died on June 9, 1837.

After a plaster cast had been made of her face, the body was placed in a leaden coffin and was buried in a cemetery on the outskirts of Rome. When Anna Maria's popularity became widespread and miracles were occurring through her intercession, her body was removed to the city in 1855, eighteen years after burial. Discovered incorrupt, it was still intact three years later when it was placed in the Basilica of San Chrysogono. The body is no longer incorrupt, but the bones are well arranged and enclosed in a representative figure clothed in the habit of a Trinitarian tertiary. This is seen in a glass-sided reliquary beneath an altar of the basilica. Also found there is a small museum containing articles the beata used during her life.

Among those who testified during the Process of Beatification was her husband, Domenico, who survived Anna Maria by sixteen years. The ninety-two-year-old Domenico gave his wife a glowing tribute, as did two daughters who gave evidence of their mother's heroic virtues.

Anna Maria was beatified on May 30, 1920 by Pope Benedict XV, who later designated her a special protectress of mothers.

SIX

BLESSED CASTORA GABRIELLI

D. 1391

DESCRIBED as being exceedingly beautiful and of a sweet, retiring disposition, Castora was a member of a prominent family of Gubbio, Italy. Her father was Count Petruccio Gabrielli; her mother was a sister of Paul Gabrielli, a bishop of Lucca.

In obedience to her parents, Castora married a man of her own rank, Gualterio Sanfaraneo, a doctor of laws, whose home was at St. Angelo in Vado. Soon after their marriage, her husband proved to be a man of violent temper and unbearable disposition. Castora had much to suffer, but she bore all her trials with true Christian patience. When her household chores were completed, she spent the remaining time in prayer, pleading for her husband's change of heart and begging for all the graces she needed in order to endure the unhappiness of her state.

Castora's only child, a son named Oddo, grew up to be an upright and pious man as the result of his mother's training and example.

After her husband's death, Castora became a tertiary in the Franciscan Third Order. With one of the ideals of the order being that of poverty, Castora decided to sell all her possessions and to give the proceeds to the poor. Her virtuous son agreed to the sale and joined in his mother's generosity.

Bl. Castora spent her days in prayer and penance until her death in 1391. She first was buried at Macerata, but through the efforts of her son, her relics were brought back to St. Angelo in Vado, where they were laid to rest in the Church of St. Francis, the church in which she had so often prayed for her husband during the days of her unhappy marriage.

SEVEN

SAINT CATHERINE
OF GENOA

1447–1510

THE Fieschi family of Italy distinguished itself in its long history by giving to the Church a cardinal and two popes, Innocent IV and Adrian V. Another member of the family, Jacopo Fieschi, who was the Viceroy of Naples for King Rene of Anjou, married Francesca di Negro. They were parents of five children; the last, born in 1447, was a daughter whom the Church recognizes as St. Catherine of Genoa.

The three sons and two daughters of the family were afforded all the advantages of their father's prestigious position and their mother's noble family. Despite the many privileges offered them, the two girls turned their wholehearted attention to the devout practices of their faith. Catherine's sister, Limbania, entered the religious life as a canoness regular, but when Catherine attempted to join her sister, her entrance was delayed because of her youth. The following year, 1461, Catherine's father died. Soon afterward there began a political realignment between two of Italy's politically important families, the Guelph Fieschi family and that of the Ghibelline Adorno. The union of the two families was settled when, on January 13, 1463, at the age of sixteen, the pious Catherine

Fieschi was married to Giuliano Adorno.

The two were different in temperament, character and ideals. Catherine, in addition to being physically beautiful, was intelligent, caring, modest, thrifty, sensitive to the needs of others, deeply religious, and of an even temperament. Giuliano was pleasure-loving, self-indulgent, undisciplined, hot-tempered, a spendthrift, and—by his own admission— an unfaithful husband. It is no wonder then, with the clash of these two personalities, that Catherine was unhappy. Since her husband was seldom at home, Catherine spent the first five years of her marriage in virtual solitude and sadness. During the next five years, Catherine unsuccessfully attempted to relieve her inner depression and desperation by engaging in the gaieties and the recreations of the world. Throughout her unhappy state, Catherine never lost her trust in God, and she continued all the practices of her religion.

After enduring years of intense unhappiness, Catherine was rewarded by God with an experience that occurred on March 20, 1473. One contemporary biographer claims she was making her confession, another that she was kneeling before a priest for his blessing, when she was suddenly over- come by grace and an immense love of God. Lifted above her miseries, Catherine was thereafter radically changed. A few days later she was granted a vision of the Crucified. After making a general confession of her sins, she became a daily communicant, which was a rare practice at the time.

Almost simultaneously with the transformation in Catherine's life, her husband's life was also changed. After liv- ing for years in extravagance and self-indulgence, Guiliano's financial situation became so desperate that he was on the verge

34

of bankruptcy. This misfortune, together with Catherine's prayers, resulted in his complete conversion. He agreed to a life of perpetual continence and joined the Franciscan Third Order. Although Catherine admired the Franciscans, she never seemed inclined to imitate her husband in this respect, but did join him in practicing one of the ideals of the order, that of poverty.

The couple moved from their palazzo into a small, humble house in a poorer section of the city and devoted themselves to the care of the poor of the area, as well as of the sick in the Hospital of Pammatone. For six years they continued in this situation, until they were invited to live in the hospital itself. From the year 1479, when the couple moved into the hospital, until 1490, Catherine worked as an ordinary nurse, but in 1490 she began serving as the hospital's administrator, and later she worked as its treasurer.

Catherine's sanctity and tireless heroism in the service of God's poor was exemplified during the plague of 1493, when it is estimated that eighty percent of the city's population perished. During this plague Catherine is said to have contracted the fever from a dying woman whom she had impulsively kissed. She recovered from the fever, but her overall health suffered from then on, making it necessary for her to resign as administrator of the hospital in 1496, after having served six years in that capacity.

The following year Giuliano died following a painful illness. Catherine reputedly said to a friend, "Messer Giuliano is gone, and as you know well, he was of a rather wayward nature, so that I suffered much interiorly. But my tender love assured me of his salvation before he had yet passed from this life." In his will Giuliano provided for his illegitimate daughter Thobia and her unnamed mother. In her charity and thoughtfulness, Catherine made herself responsible for seeing that Thobia should never be in want or neglected, and since she had no children of her own, Catherine became, as it were, Thobia's adopted mother.

During much of her life, Catherine's spirituality developed solely under the influence of grace. But then, shortly after her husband's death, she benefited from the spiritual direction of the priest, Cattaneo Marabotto, to whom the Church is indebted for his writings on the saint's spirit, doctrine, mystical experiences and interior life. Catherine was ever mindful of temporal necessities and continued nursing the sick and managing the details of her husband's estate. She was also quite busy advising and instructing the many people who were attracted by her spiritual teaching.

Catherine suffered for many years from various ailments until at length, in 1507, her health gave way completely. One of her physicians was the doctor of King Henry VII of England, but he and other physicians were unable to diagnose her condition. They eventually decided that her ailments had supernatural origins, since she lacked all the symptoms that they could recognize. Finally, on September 15, 1510, "This blessed soul gently breathed her last in great peace and tranquility and flew to her tender and much-desired Love."

Burial was in the hospital chapel. Eighteen months later, when the body was exhumed to be placed in a marble sepulchre, it was found perfectly preserved, in spite of excessive dampness. In response to popular demand, the body was exposed for eight days. Immediately, cures attributed to

Catherine's intercession began to take place, and veneration of the saint began and continued from that time onward. Moved a number of times, the body was placed in a glass-sided shrine in the year 1694, the same reliquary in which it is still exposed. The incorrupt body was carefully examined by physicians in 1960. They recorded after their inspection: "The conservation is truly exceptional and surprising and deserves an analysis of the cause. The surprise of the faithful is justified when they attribute this to a supernatural cause." The relic in its glass-sided reliquary is now located high atop the main altar of the church built in St. Catherine's honor in Genoa, Italy.

The saint's thoughts, sayings and spiritual insights are contained in two books, the *Treatise on Purgatory* and the *Spiritual Dialogue*. The Holy Office declared that these two works were enough to prove her sanctity.

Catherine was canonized by Pope Clement XII in 1737; she received that honor together with St. Vincent de Paul, St. Francis Regis, and St. Giuliana Falconieri.

EIGHT

SAINT CLOTILDE

474–545

CLOTILDE was born in Lyon, France, about the year 474 to Chilperic, the ruler of the Burgundians of Lyon, and Caretana, a fervent Catholic. When Clotilde's father died, her mother took the sixteen-year-old girl and her sister Sendeleuba to Geneva. Sendeleuba eventually took the veil in the convent of St. Victor at Geneva, but Clotilde became the bride of Clovis, King of the Salian Franks, when she was about eighteen years old.

The wedding took place at Soissons, which Clovis had made his new capital. Although Clovis was a pagan, he—like his father—maintained a friendly relationship with the bishops of the realm, especially with St. Remigius, Archbishop of Rheims. St. Remigius previously had sent Clovis a warm letter of congratulations when he had ascended the throne at the age of fifteen.

Clotilde exercised great influence over her husband and tried every means to convert him to the Faith. Although Clovis resisted and continued in his pagan beliefs, he did permit Clotilde to baptize their first child, a son named Ingomar, who died in infancy. He likewise permitted the Baptism of the other children: Clodomir, Childebert, Clotaire, and a daughter who bore her mother's name.

Clovis' decision to become a Christian was made dramatically on the field of battle when he was in the process of losing to the Alemanni. When his troops were on the verge of yielding to the enemy, Clovis turned for help to Clotilde's God, promising to accept the Faith if he were victorious. The tide of the conflict took a miraculous turn; the battle was won, and on Christmas morning, 496, Clovis was baptized with great pomp by St. Remigius in Rheims Cathedral. His sister Abofledis and 3,000 of his Franks were also received into the Church at the same time.

Clovis was also successful in further conquests in Gaul. Clotilde no doubt was happy with this accomplishment, which furnished fresh fields for extending the Catholic faith. Together, Clovis and Clotilde founded in Paris the Church of the Apostles Peter and Paul, which was to serve them as a mausoleum and which was afterwards renamed for St. Genevieve. In this church Clotilde buried her husband, Clovis, when he died in 511. The couple had been married nineteen years.

While the years previous to Clovis' death were relatively happy ones, Clotilde's widowhood was saddened by family feuds and the problems of her three sons and daughter.

The first problem involving Clotilde's children concerned her daughter, the princess Clotilde, whose husband, the Visigoth Amalaric, was abusing her. So cruel and inhuman was his behavior, as reported in the news that reached the rest of the family, that St. Clotilde's son Childebert was outraged. Rising to the defense of his sister, he gathered together an army, battled against Amalaric, defeated him and put him to death. Childebert was in the process of bringing his sister home when she died on the journey as a result of the harsh treatment she had endured at the hands of her husband. We can only imagine St. Clotilde's grief upon receiving the body of her only daughter.

Another difficulty involved Clotilde's son, Clodomir, who attacked his cousin St. Sigismund, captured him and mercilessly put him to death, together with his wife and children. Later, Clodomir was himself killed in retaliation by St. Sigismund's brother Godomar in the battle of Vezeronce in the year 542.

Following the death of Clodomir, St. Clotilde adopted his three little sons, intending to raise them as her own children. Her two remaining sons, Clotaire and Childebert, decided to acquire undisputed possession of their deceased brother's inheritance, which they divided between themselves. Knowing that their three little nephews, who were the rightful heirs, presented a hindrance to their greed, the two brothers—under the pretense of wanting their nephews to visit them—persuaded St. Clotilde to send the children to them. No sooner had the children arrived than Clotaire, with his own hand, killed two of the children, who were ten and seven years of age. The youngest child, Clodoald, escaped and afterwards became a monk near Paris, at the monastery of Nogent, which later was renamed St. Cloud in his honor.

Brokenhearted at the loss of her two grandsons, plus the knowledge that her two sons had plotted the murders and that one had actually performed the deed, St. Clotilde left Paris and moved to Tours. There she spent the rest of her life in helping the poor and suffering and in praying at the tomb of St. Martin, to whom she had a great devotion.

While at Tours, St. Clotilde learned that her two sons, Childebert and Clotaire, had been feuding and were on the verge of battle. In her anguish, St. Clotilde spent the whole night in prayer before St. Martin's shrine, begging God to put an end to the conflict. The saint's prayers were answered the very next day, when the armies were facing each other on the field of battle. Before the conflict could begin, a storm arose with such turbulence that the troops scattered for safety.

A month later, St. Clotilde was seized with a serious ailment. She died at the age of about seventy-one, having been a widow for thirty-four years. The two sons who had caused their mother so much grief buried St. Clotilde beside her husband and children in the Church of the Apostles, which Clotilde and Clovis had built many years before. The church was later renamed after St. Genevieve, the patroness of Paris.

NINE

SAINT DOROTHEA
OF MONTAU

1347–1394

FROM the age of seventeen until she was thirty-five years of age, this saint suffered prolonged grief and unhappiness. Born in 1347 of poor parents at Montau (Marienburg), Germany, Dorothea was married at the age of seventeen to Albert, a sword smith of Danzig, by whom she had nine children. The youngest child, a daughter, eventually became a Benedictine nun, but the rest all died during their childhood. The grief that Dorothea experienced at the loss of her children was alleviated only by the grace and comforts of her faith. Her husband offered her little or no consolation; in fact, while their children were sick and dying, she had much to suffer from Albert, who was ill-tempered and overbearing. For most of her married life, Dorothea had much to endure on this account.

Eventually, however, her gentleness and patience affected his disposition to such an extent that in 1382, after almost twenty years of married life, Albert agreed to accompany his pious wife on a pilgrimage to Aachen. The change in Albert was so dramatic that he began to share his wife's spiritual life and readily agreed to accompany her on other pilgrimages. Together the couple prayed at a number of shrines, including

Einsiedeln and Cologne. They were planning a journey to Rome when Albert became ill, but at his insistence Dorothea went alone. Upon her return, she learned that her husband had just died.

Widowed at the age of forty-three, Dorothea moved to Marienwerder, and in 1393, with the approval of her confessor, she took up residence in a cell by the church of the Teutonic Knights. She was there only a year, but during that time she gained a great reputation for holiness. Many were the visitors who came to her asking for advice in temporal and spiritual matters, and many were those who came to her hoping for a physical cure. We are told by her spiritual director, who wrote her *Life*, that Dorothea had a very intense devotion to the Blessed Sacrament and was often supernaturally enabled to look upon it.

Dorothea was greatly revered by the people who knew her; they acclaimed her a saint immediately after her death in 1394.

Devotion to St. Dorothea spread to Poland, Lithuania, Bohemia, and elsewhere. Unfortunately, the church at Marienwerder where Dorothea was buried was seized by the Lutherans. Since then, her relics have not been found.

TEN

SAINT ELIZABETH, QUEEN OF PORTUGAL

1271–1336

ELIZABETH (or Isabel) was born in 1271 to Peter III, King of Aragon, Spain, and Constantia, daughter of Manfred, King of Sicily. Her grandfather was Emperor Frederick II; her great-aunt was none other than the great St. Elizabeth of Hungary, who had been canonized by Pope Gregory IX in 1235, only thirty-five years before the birth of her namesake.

The young princess was of a sweet disposition, and from her early years she was attracted to prayer and virtue. At the age of eight she began to fast and to practice self-denial, although those who cared for her cautioned against such practices for fear that her health would be jeopardized.

At the tender age of twelve she was married to Denis, King of Portugal, who admired her beauty and personality. Although he did not feel inclined to imitate Elizabeth's devotions, he allowed her full liberty to spend her time and income as she pleased. Given this freedom, she arranged her time with great care and rarely interrupted her schedule except for extraordinary reasons. She rose very early every morning and recited Matins, Lauds, and Prime before she attended

Holy Mass. Certain hours during the day were allotted to her domestic affairs, public business and charities. In the afternoon she again spent time in prayer before the recitation of Vespers. Her food was simple, her dress was modest, and her conversation was humble and pleasant.

Elizabeth was particularly attracted to relieving the poor, and she gave orders that all pilgrims and poor strangers should be given shelter and necessities. She visited and served the sick and founded in different parts of the kingdom many charitable establishments, particularly a hospital near her own palace at Coimbra. She established a house for penitent women at Torres Novas, as well as a refuge for foundlings. She also provided marriage dowries for girls who were poor. Although busy with many projects, she did not neglect her immediate duties, and she gave her husband respect, love, and obedience.

Whether Denis lost interest in his wife because of her multiple devotions and works of charity, or whether he would have turned away from her regardless, we do not know for certain. But we are informed that while he was a good ruler and was devoted to his realm, in private he was selfish, sinful, and dissolute.

The saint tried every means to reclaim her husband and she grieved deeply for the scandal that he gave to the people. She never ceased praying for him or asking the prayers of others for his conversion. She showed great courtesy and patience during this trial and lovingly cared for Denis' illegitimate children, providing for their present and future welfare. When the ladies of the court reproached her for treating her husband's faults too leniently, the saint replied, "If the King sins, am I to lose patience and thus add my transgressions to his? I love better to confide my sorrows to God and His holy saints and to strive to win back my husband by gentleness."

A story is told of an incident which, if it actually happened, probably contributed to the King's conversion. The Queen had a page who faithfully and secretly distributed her donations to the poor when she was unable to do so herself. Another page, envious that he was not given this assignment, reported to the King that the Queen had an excessive fondness for this fellow page and that he performed secret functions for her.

Denis believed the report, and because of his jealousy, arranged with the lime-burner that on a certain day he should throw into the kiln the first page who should arrive with a royal message. On the day appointed, Denis sent the Queen's page to the lime-kiln, but when the page passed a church, he stopped to attend Holy Mass, as was his custom. This delay saved him. The King then sent the informer to verify the outcome of the plan. He arrived first and was burned to death. The Queen's page, after finishing his prayers, passed the lime-kiln and brought back word to the King that his order had been fulfilled. The King saw in this twist of events that God, because of the Holy Mass, had vindicated the honor of the Queen.

St. Elizabeth had two children, Alfonso, who afterward succeeded his father, and a daughter, Constantia. Alfonso showed a very rebellious spirit when he grew up, due in part to the favor in which his father held his illegitimate sons. In 1323, Alfonso declared war against his illegitimate brothers and the King. Queen Elizabeth re-established peace and a reconciliation after finding it necessary to ride out on horseback between the opposing forces. Pope John XXII wrote in praise of her efforts, but many suggested to the King that Elizabeth secretly favored her own son, and for a time she was banished from the court.

When Denis became seriously ill, Elizabeth never left him except for her attendance at church services. She served and attended him with great patience and devotion during his long and tedious illness and had many Masses offered for his complete repentance. The Queen's prayers were answered when Denis expressed sincere sorrow for the errors of his life and died a holy death.

Elizabeth made a pilgrimage to Compostella to pray for her husband's soul and then spent a period of mourning at the convent of the Poor Clares which she had founded at Coimbra. She herself never joined the community, but she was professed in the Third Order of St. Francis. She lived in a house which she built near the convent and often visited the nuns, frequently serving them at table. One of her companions during this time was her daughter-in-law, Queen Beatrice.

Always devoted to maintaining peace, St. Elizabeth once averted a war between Ferdinand IV of Castile and his cousin, who had laid claim to the crown. She again acted as peacemaker when the same prince challenged her own brother, James II of Aragon. Unfortunately, her efforts to save the lives of countless men ironically caused her own death.

In 1336 Elizabeth's son, now Alfonso IV, set out on an expedition against his son-in-law, the King of Castile, who had married Alfonso's daughter Maria and had neglected and abused her. Elizabeth prepared to meet and reconcile the two kings—against the advice of her servants, who cautioned her to postpone her journey on account of the heat. But stating that she could find no better way to risk her health than by seeking to prevent the miseries of war, Elizabeth left for Estremoz, where her son was camped.

Although very ill and knowing that her death was not far off, Elizabeth was successful in reconciling the two sovereigns. Shortly thereafter she confessed and received Holy Viaticum and the Last Rites of the Church. Calling upon the most holy Mother of God, she died peacefully in the presence of her son and daughter-in-law. She was buried in the church of the Poor Clare monastery at Coimbra, which she honored after her death with many miracles.

Queen Elizabeth of Portugal was canonized by Pope Urban VIII in 1625.

ELEVEN

SAINT ELZEAR AND BLESSED DELPHINA

D. 1323 / D. 1358

SOON after Elzear was born, his mother took him in her arms and offered him to God with great fervor. She begged that he might never offend His Divine Majesty, but might rather die in his infancy than live to commit a serious sin. His mother's prayers were answered, since later in life St. Elzear acknowledged that he had never committed a mortal sin. The lessons in virtue which he had received from his mother were perfected by his uncle, William of Sabran, abbot of St. Victor's at Marseille. It was in that monastery that Elzear was educated.

Having been born in Provence, France, in the year 1285, Elzear was still a child when Charles II, King of Sicily, arranged Elzear's engagement to Delphina, daughter and heiress to the Lord of Puy-Michel. Delphina was an orphan. Like her intended, who was educated by an uncle who was an abbot, Delphina was educated by her aunt who was an abbess. When Elzear and Delphina were both about fifteen years old, their marriage took place at Chateau-Pont-Michel.

It is claimed by at least one biographer that the couple decided, on their wedding night, to live as brother and sister.

And it is known that in 1315, in the chapel of their castle, after they received Holy Communion, they stood at the foot of the altar and publicly pronounced their vows of perpetual continence. This is claimed by some to indicate that both were inclined toward a religious vocation, but entered into the marriage state under obedience to the advice of their elders.

Elzear was twenty-three years old when he inherited his father's honors and estates. He became the Baron of Ansouis in Provence and Count of Ariano in the kingdom of Naples. When Elzear had to journey to Italy to take possession of the lordship of Ariano, he found the Italians poorly disposed toward him as a Frenchman. Then, when a rebellion was threatened, Elzear's cousin, the Prince of Taranto, advised him to subdue the rebels with executions and force of arms—a course of action which Elzear refused to take. Instead of pursuing a confrontation, Elzear spent three years in opposing the rebellion with tact, gentleness, meekness, and patience. His friends reproachfully accused him of being indolent and cowardly, but in the end the rebels abandoned their effort. With submission and respect, they invited the saint to take possession of his territory.

In explaining why he bore the insults, injuries and difficulties with patience, Elzear explained, "If I receive any affront or feel impatience begin to arise in my breast, I turn all my thoughts toward Jesus Christ crucified and say to myself: Can what I suffer bear any comparison with what Jesus Christ was pleased to undergo for me?"

Elzear once again countered insults with patience and forgiveness when he was going through papers that had been left by his father. Several letters were found that had been written by a certain gentleman who suggested that Elzear should be disinherited because he was more of a monk than a soldier. When Delphina read the insults and criticisms that were also mentioned in the letter, she expressed the hope that her husband would deal with the writer as he deserved. But Elzear reminded her that Christ commands us not to seek revenge but to forgive injuries and to overcome hatred with charity. He destroyed the letters and never spoke of them again. When the gentleman came to him, not knowing that Elzear had read his letters, Elzear greeted him affectionately and won his friendship.

The gentleman was wrong in his opinion of Elzear. While the saint had the virtues and demeanor of a monk, he was also a soldier, having taken up arms in Italy on behalf of the Guelph party. With his followers he helped to drive Emperor Henry VII from Rome in 1312.

Elzear exercised charity in a number of areas. He visited prisoners who were condemned to death, converted many with tender words and secretly aided widows, orphans and the poor. He recited the Divine Office every day and communicated almost as often. He once said to Delphina, "I do not think that any man on earth can enjoy a happiness equal to that which I have in Holy Communion." In one of his letters to her he wrote, "You want to hear often of me. Go then and visit our loving Lord Jesus in the Blessed Sacrament, and enter in spirit into His Sacred Heart. You will always find me there."

While Elzear was devout and spent much time in prayer, he did not neglect the temporal concerns of his position. Diligent in the care of his household, he drew up the following regulations:

Everyone in my family shall daily hear Mass, whatever business he may have. If God be well served, nothing will be wanting. . . . Let no persons be idle. In the morning a little time shall be allowed for meditation, but away with those who are perpetually in the church to avoid doing their work. This they do, not because they love contemplation, but because they want to have their work done for them. . . . When a difference or quarrel arises, let the scriptural precept be observed that it be composed before the sun goes down. I know the impossibility of living among men and not having something to suffer. Scarcely a man is in tune with himself one whole day; but not to be willing to bear with or pardon others is diabolical, and to love enemies and to render good for evil is the touchstone of the sons of God. . . . I strictly command that no officer or servant under my jurisdiction or authority injure any man in goods, honor or reputation, or oppress any poor person, or damage anyone under color of doing my business. I do not want my castle to be a cloister or my people hermits. Let them be merry, and enjoy recreation at the right times, but not with a bad conscience or with danger of transgressing against God.

St. Elzear himself set the example in everything that he prescribed to others, and Bl. Delphina concurred with her husband in all his views and was perfectly obedient to him. Although strictly observing their vow of chastity, they were nevertheless perfectly suited to one another. They were warm, affectionate, and caring, while harmony and peace held sway in their dealings with one another and in their household.

When King Robert of Naples sent St. Elzear to Paris to ask for the hand of Mary of Valois for King Robert's son, Bl. Delphina was concerned for her husband amid the dangers of the Parisian court. Elzear observed that since, by the grace of God, he had kept his virtue in Naples, he was not likely to come to any harm in Paris.

But a danger of another kind did await Elzear in Paris, in the form of a sickness that proved to be fatal. While he awaited death, he made a general confession and continued to confess almost every day of his illness, even though he is said never to have offended God by mortal sin. The history of Christ's Passion was read to him every day, and in this he found great comfort in spite of his pains. After receiving the Holy Eucharist for the last time, Elzear said with great joy, "This is my hope; in this I desire to die." On September 27, 1323 Elzear died in the arms of Fr. Francis Mayronis, a Franciscan friar who had been his confessor. In accord with Elzear's orders, his body was carried to Apt and there interred in the Church of the Franciscans.

Fourteen years earlier, about the year 1309, St. Elzear had assisted as godfather at the baptism of William of Grimoard, son of the Sieur de Grisac. William was a sickly child whose restoration to health was credited to the prayers of his godfather. Fifty-three years later, this William became Pope Urban V, and in 1369 he signed the decree of canonization of his godfather, Elzear, whose name is listed in the *Roman Martyrology* on September 27, the day of his death.

Bl. Delphina survived her husband by thirty-five years. She remained at the Neapolitan court until the death of Queen Sanchia, who had entered the Order of the Poor Clares. Delphina then returned to France and led the life of a recluse, first at Cabrieres and then at Apt. She distributed the proceeds of her estates to the poor, and during her last years she was afflicted with a painful illness, which she bore with admirable patience until her death. She was buried beside her husband in Apt.

Both St. Elzear and Bl. Delphina were members of the Third Order of St. Francis, and for this reason they are particularly venerated by the Franciscans.

TWELVE

SAINT GENGULPHUS

D. 760

G ENGULPHUS (or Gengoul) was a Burgundian knight who was especially admired for his bravery, his accomplishments for the Frankish kingdom, and his upright and virtuous life. He was also held in the highest regard by Pepin the Short, Mayor of the Palace of the whole Frankish kingdom and later the King of the Franks. Gengulphus was so likeable and even-tempered that he and Pepin were often found side by side.

Gengulphus eventually married a woman of rank whom he deeply loved and trusted, but soon after their marriage she proved to be scandalously unfaithful to him and unbearably ill-tempered. When corrections and appeals proved useless, the peace-loving Gengulphus made provisions for her care and withdrew to his castle in Burgundy. During his retirement from public life he led the life of a recluse, spending his time in penitential exercises and in supplying alms to the needy.

According to historical accounts, Gelgulphus was killed by his wife's paramour who, at her instigation, broke into his chamber one night and murdered him as he lay in bed.

After the wide distribution of his relics, Gengulphus was honored in Holland, Belgium and Savoy.

Since he suffered great humiliation and heartache as the result of his wife's infidelity, Gengulphus is regarded as the patron saint of those who are unhappily married.

THIRTEEN

SAINT GODELIEVE

C. 1049–1070

THE persecution and cruelty suffered by this holy saint at the hands of her husband and mother-in-law would seem almost unbelievable, had it not been recorded by a contemporary priest by the name of Drogo. From his pen, as well as others, we learn the following fantastic history of St. Godelieve.

Born about the year 1049 in the castle of Londesvoorde in the County of Boulogne, Belgium, Godelieve was the youngest of the three children born to Hemfried, Lord of Wierre-Effroy, and his wife Ogeva. During her childhood, Godelieve was accustomed to perform exercises of piety and was soon distinguished for her extraordinary virtues. The poor who flocked to her always found a generous friend, but Godelieve's efforts to help them often placed her in difficulties with her father and her father's steward.

By the time Godelieve had reached her eighteenth year, the fame of her beauty and admirable qualities had spread throughout the district. Many suitors presented themselves, but all were rejected in favor of the resolution she had made of renouncing the world for the cloister. However, one suitor, Bertolf of Gistel, would not be put off. Apparently driven by an egotistical necessity to win where others had failed, he appealed to her father's suzerain, Eustache II, Count of Boulogne, whose influence proved successful in persuading Godelieve to marry.

Following the wedding ceremony, Bertolf and his bride journeyed to Gistel. There the young bride found a bitter and unrelenting enemy in Bertolf's mother, who influenced her son to abandon his new wife on the very day of their arrival. Godelieve was given over to the care of her mother-in-law, who was not content with petty persecutions, but treated her with "fanatic brutality." Apparently the mother had other plans for her son and was furious that he had disregarded them in favor of this girl from Boulogne. Godelieve's mother-in-law not only heaped abuse on her, but she also placed her in a narrow cell with barely enough nourishment to support life. It was apparent that the mother-in-law wanted to be rid of her, but she dared not kill Godelieve directly. As though her sufferings, both mental and physical, were not enough, Godelieve's husband, under the influence of his mother, would not go near his bride, and he spread scandalous stories about her.

After a time, Godelieve succeeded in escaping to her father's house. Her unexpected return, together with her poor physical condition, alarmed Hemfried. He ordered Godelieve, under obedience, to confide to him the conditions under which she had been living. Although Godelieve wanted to spare her husband, she was nevertheless forced under obedience and respect for her father to tell all that had occurred at her husband's home. After Godelieve had revealed the cruelty of her existence there, her father was so outraged that he reported the matter to the Bishop of Tournai, as well as to the Count of Flanders. These threatened Bertolf with the terrors of the Church and State. It was ruled that Bertolf should reconcile with his wife and in the future treat her with respect.

Seemingly repentant, Bertolf promised to restore his wife to her rightful position in his household and to treat her with gentleness. But Godelieve's return to Gistel was met with renewed persecution in a vain attempt to ruin her health and finish her life.

Bertolf resorted to more direct action in the year 1070. He pretended a complete change of heart and a desire for reconciliation—this with the intention of averting the suspicion of the crime he was contemplating. Then, after instructing two servants on what they were to do, Bertolf left for the City of Bruges. While he was gone, Godelieve was tricked one dark night into stepping outside her home by a back door. Once she was outside, the two servants seized her; placing a thong tightly around her neck, they took her to a nearby pond, where they held her head beneath the water until she was dead. Intending the death to appear to have been from natural causes, they placed Godelieve's body back in her bed, but the marks about her neck revealed the criminal cause of her death. Since her husband was far away at the time, Godelieve's father could not place a claim against him.

Bertolf soon married for a second time, but the daughter of this marriage, Edith, was born blind. A miraculous recovery of sight took place when her eyes were bathed in the water taken from the pool where Godelieve had died. This miracle so affected Bertolf that he experienced a true conversion. He journeyed to Rome to obtain absolution for the murder of Godelieve, finally entering the monastery of St. Winoc at Bruges, where he expiated his sins by a life of severe penance.

At Bertolf's request, his daughter Edith erected a Benedictine Abbey at Gistel. This abbey experienced various damages and repairs throughout the centuries. In 1953 important alterations were made. When these were completed, the Abbey St. Godelieve was solemnly consecrated on June 26 of that year. The abbey, which is still in the care of the Benedictine nuns, is also known as the Abbey Ten Putte, the "Abbey by the Well," since a well is maintained there that has the same water found in the pool in which Godelieve died. The well is at the place where Edith received her sight.

Following Godelieve's death, God confirmed her virtues by so many miracles that her body was exhumed in 1084 by the Bishop of Tournai for enshrinement in the church. A copy of the formal verification of the saint's relics made at that time, fourteen years after Godelieve's death, has been preserved. This verification of the relics was found when the shrine was solemnly visited and examined in 1907. The saint's relics, recognized at various times by ecclesiastical authority, are to be found in various cities of Belgium, but important relics of the saint are still kept in the church of the abbey.

At the place where Godelieve was murdered there stands a statue of the saint which has been revered by pilgrims for centuries. Also of interest to pilgrims is the Little Cellar, or Prison of Godelieve, which is found in the basement of the abbey's south wing. This is the place where Godelieve withstood abuse and neglect—so heroically that she has been regarded as "the most blessed woman in Flanders."

St. Godelieve has always been depicted with four crowns,

a unique iconographical feature. These crowns are the symbols of her virginity, her marriage, her repudiation (which is regarded as the equivalent to widowhood), and her martyrdom.

The saint is invoked at the abbey during the whole year, but especially during the annual solemnities which take place between July 6 and July 30. Her intercession is particularly sought in cases of eye or throat disorders and for maintaining or re-establishing peace in families.

FOURTEEN

SAINT GORGONIA

D. 374

S T. GREGORY Nazianzus the Elder and his wife St. Nonna had three children: St. Gregory Nazianzen, the great Doctor of the Church; St. Caesarius, a physician by profession; and St. Gorgonia, who was the eldest. Gorgonia married a man from Iconium named Vitalian; they had three children, whom Gorgonia brought up with the same care that she had received from her parents.

What we know of St. Gorgonia is given to us by her brother St. Gregory Nazianzen in the funeral oration he delivered at the time of her death. This eulogy, still extant, is very lengthy in praise of her virtuous life. St. Gregory begins the eulogy in this way:

> In praising my sister, I shall be honoring my own family. Yet while she is a member of my family I shall not on that account praise her falsely, but because what is true is for that reason praiseworthy. Moreover, this truth is not only well-founded, but also well-known.

After speaking of her many virtues, St. Gregory tells the following about Gorgonia's exemplary marriage:

> Though she was linked in carnal union, she was not on that

account separated from the Spirit, nor because she had her husband as her head did she ignore her first Head. When she had served the world and nature a little, to the extent that the law of the flesh willed it, or, rather, He who imposed this law on the flesh, she consecrated herself wholly to God. And what is most excellent and honorable, she also won over her husband and gained, instead of an unreasonable master, a good fellow servant. Not only that, she also made the fruit of her body, her children and her children's children, the fruit of her spirit, and dedicated to God, instead of her single soul, her whole family and household. And she rendered marriage itself laudable by her pleasing and acceptable life in wedlock and by the fair fruit of her union. And she exhibited herself, as long as she lived, as an exemplar of every excellence to her children.

St. Gregory Nazianzen speaks of the saint's great humility and modesty and gives a lesson to those who are overly fond of outward appearances:

She was never adorned with gold fashioned by art into surpassing beauty, or with fair tresses fully or partly exposed, or with spiral curls, or with the ingenious arrangements of those who disgracefully turn the noble head into a showpiece. Hers were no costly, flowing, diaphanous robes, hers no brilliant and beautiful gems, flashing color round about and causing the figure to glow with light. . . . But while she was familiar with the many and various external ornaments of women, she recognized none as more precious than her own character and the splendor which lies within. The only red that pleased her was the blush of modesty, and the only pallor, that which comes from abstinence. But pigments and makeup and living pictures and flowing beauty of form she left to the women of the stage and the public squares, and to all for whom it is a disgrace and a reproach to feel ashamed.

We are told that St. Gorgonia "was known as a counselor

not only of her family . . . but also of all those about her, who regarded her suggestions and recommendations as law." She also gave a courteous and generous welcome to all who came to her in God's name, particularly travelers, the blind, the lame, widows and orphans. "Her house," we are told, "was a common hospice for all her needy relatives, and her goods were as common to all the needy as their own personal belongings." We are also informed that she frequently fasted and spent many evenings in fervent prayer.

To demonstrate his sister's great confidence in God, St. Gregory Nazianzen tells us of an incident in the life of the saint: It was well known by her neighbors that she was riding one day in her carriage when the mules pulling it went out of control. During the chase the carriage overturned and

> she was dragged along horribly and suffered serious injuries
> . . . Although crushed and mangled internally and externally
> in bone and limb, she would have no physician save Him
> who had permitted the accident. . . . Nor from anyone else
> but Him did she obtain her restoration. Although her suffer-
> ing was human, her recovery was supernatural, and she gave
> to posterity a compelling argument for the display of faith in
> affliction and patient endurance in misfortune.

When the accident first occurred, Gorgonia's neighbors were scandalized that such a terrible thing should happen to someone who was so virtuous. But they were amazed at her unexpected recovery, and "they believed that the tragedy had happened for the very reason that she might be glorified by her sufferings."

Another time the saint became seriously ill with a strange ailment that St. Gregory said did not seem human. "Nor did the skill of physicians who carefully examined the case, both singly and in consultation, prove of any avail." The disease seems to have presented itself at frequent intervals with a fever, coma, pallor, and a paralysis of mind and body. When Gorgonia realized that the physicians could not help her, she visited the church (when the disease had somewhat abated) and prostrated herself with faith at the altar. Then she performed what St. Gregory calls "an act of pious and noble impudence." She placed her head on the altar "and pouring abundant tears upon it, as she who had once watered the feet of Christ, she vowed that she would not loose her hold until she obtained her recovery." After receiving the Body and Blood of Our Lord, she felt herself completely recovered, and "went away relieved in body and soul and mind. . ."

When the time for her death approached, St. Gorgonia "enjoined on her husband, her children and her friends such precepts as befitted one so full of love . . . and she discoursed beautifully on the future life, making her last day a day of solemn festival." St. Gorgonia's holy passing, in the arms of her mother, St. Nonna, greatly edified all who gathered about her bed. St. Gorgonia died in the year 374. Her feast day was formerly observed on December 9.

FIFTEEN

SAINT GUMMARUS

D. 774

A S THE son of the Lord of Emblehem, Belgium, Gummarus served in the court of Pepin the Short, where he demonstrated the results of his youthful training in the Faith by being humble, honest, exact in his duties and fervent in all the exercises of devotion. Although Pepin was occupied with ambitious endeavors, he greatly admired the virtues of his courtier and raised him to a high position with added responsibilities.

Presumably as a reward for his faithfulness, Pepin proposed a match between Gummarus and a lady of noble birth named Gwinmarie. Both parties consented and the marriage was solemnized. However, soon after the wedding Gwinmarie displayed her true temperament. According to the description handed down to us, she was extravagant, proud, capricious, impatient, incorrigible, unteachable, and had a tiresome and frightful disposition.

The devout and patient Gummarus suffered terribly from the trials which his wife continually presented. With heroic virtue, Gummarus attempted for several years to encourage his wife toward more controlled behavior, but without result. Finally, Gummarus was granted a reprieve of sorts when he was asked by King Pepin to accompany, him in his wars: first in Lombardy, then in Saxony, and again in Aquitaine. Gummarus was absent for eight years. Upon his return home he found that his wife had created complete disorder and confusion in his household, and that almost all of his servants, vassals, and tenants had suffered from her overbearing oppression. Losing no time, Gummarus corrected his affairs and made restitution to all who had suffered.

Eventually, Gummarus' patience and kindness seemed to correct his wife's disposition. She seemed sincerely ashamed of her past conduct, and for a time she appeared to be truly penitent. This was only temporary, however, since she reverted to her old faults, which seemed to be even more serious than before. Gummarus tried once more to influence her, but at length he had to admit that this was impossible. By mutual consent the two separated.

Gummarus lived for a time in a cell near their home, but later he set off on a pilgrimage to Rome. He got no further than Nivesdonck; there he built himself a hermitage and lived alone for some years, until his holy death about the year 774. Afterwards, his hermitage became a place of pilgrimage. St. Gummarus is venerated at Lier, which is near the village of his birth.

SIXTEEN

SAINT HEDWIG

D. 1243

ST. HEDWIG was one of eight children born at the Castle of Andechs to Count Berthold IV. The vocations of the saint's brothers and sisters indicate the religious atmosphere in which the family was raised. Of Hedwig's four brothers, two became bishops: Ekbert of Bambert and Berthold of Aquileia. Of her sisters, Gertrude married and became the mother of the great St. Elizabeth of Hungary, while another sister, Mechtilde, became abbess of the convent at Kitzingen. Hedwig herself became a canonized saint.

Hedwig was educated in the convent of Kitzingen, and according to an old biography, she was twelve years old in 1186 when she married Henry I of Silesia, Poland. At the time of the marriage, Henry was eighteen years old. When Henry succeeded his father as Duke of Silesia in 1202, Hedwig began to play a prominent part in her husband's administration. Her prudence and piety greatly influenced the government of the land, and she was successful in maintaining peace among the nobles within her area of influence. She gave her support to new monastic foundations and assisted those already in existence.

It was chiefly through the monasteries that German

71

civilization was spread in Silesia. Together, Henry and Hedwig founded several religious houses and invited the Cistercians, Dominicans, and Franciscans into their territory. Henry founded the Hospital of the Holy Ghost at Breslau, and Hedwig tended leper women in the hospital at Newmarkt. The first religious house for women in Silesia was founded by Henry in 1202, this being a convent for Cistercian nuns at Trebnitz (Trzebnica).

For some years after her marriage, Hedwig resided chiefly at Breslau. There she gave birth to seven children. Hedwig suffered one of the most painful afflictions that can befall a mother when three of her children died in early childhood. Another three died as adults during the saint's lifetime.

After the birth of their last child, Hedwig and her husband pronounced a vow of chastity before the bishop of Breslau. Their marriage continued for another thirty years, during which Duke Henry never wore gold, silver, or purple and never shaved his beard. Because of this he was surnamed Henry the Bearded.

The couple's two sons, Henry and Conrad, were the occasion of a good deal of trouble. In 1212 Duke Henry divided his duchies between them, but on terms which were not pleasing to Conrad. Hedwig supported the cause of Henry, who was the elder. The two brothers, notwithstanding their mother's efforts to reconcile them, went into battle; Henry won decisively over his younger brother, who fled the territory. Henry eventually succeeded to his father's title. Conrad died while still a young man, as a result of a fall from his horse while hunting.

Besides the deaths of her children, Hedwig had other

trials which greatly afflicted her. In the year 1227, her husband was wounded when he was treacherously set upon by the duke of Pomerania. Hedwig immediately hastened to Gonsawa, where the bloody deed had taken place, to care for her severely wounded husband. As a result of this deed, war broke out in 1229 between Henry and Conrad of Masovia over the possession of Kraków. Conrad was defeated, but he succeeded in surprising and capturing Henry in a church while he was attending divine services. When Hedwig learned of her husband's imprisonment, she went immediately to seek his release. Her gentle manner and appearance made such an impression on Conrad of Masovia that he made peace with Henry and released him, although Conrad did ask for and obtain certain concessions.

Following the death of her husband in 1238, St. Hedwig moved to the convent of Trebnitz. Hedwig's biographers state emphatically that she did not become a member of the order, but lived there as a lay woman. She had two reasons for moving into the convent: so that she might live in a state of poverty while practicing mortification and acts of piety, and so that she could direct her vast revenues into works of charity. She is known to have attained a high degree of prayer and perfection in the convent.

A situation which developed at this time clearly indicates Hedwig's virtue and patience. The saint became acquainted with a poor old washerwoman who did not know the Our Father. Since the woman was very slow at learning the prayer, Hedwig continued instructing her for ten weeks, and even had the woman sleep in her room, so that at every spare moment they might attempt to recite it together. As a result of Hedwig's patience the old woman not only learned the prayer, but understood it as well.

Hedwig suffered yet another loss and was deeply grieved when her son Duke Henry II died at Wahlstatt in 1241 in a battle against the Tartars. Hedwig is said to have known of her son's death three days before the news reached her. She concealed her grief and controlled her tears while she consoled Henry's wife Anne, his children, and his sister Gertrude.

St. Hedwig's faith and high degree of perfection were honored by God with the gift of miracles. A nun of Trebnitz who was blind recovered her sight by the blessing of the saint, and Hedwig's biographer gives an account of several other miraculous cures obtained through her prayers. She made several predictions, in particular, one concerning her death. During her last illness, St. Hedwig insisted on being anointed before others could be convinced of the seriousness of her condition.

Hedwig was deeply loved by her people and was regarded as a saint after her death at the age of sixty-nine, in October, 1243. She was interred in the church attached to the convent. Her grave is situated to the side of the high altar; the tomb of her husband, Duke Henry I, is found in front of the altar.

Hedwig's daughter-in-law testified concerning the raptures with which Hedwig was sometimes favored, as did Herbold, her confessor, and other observers. As a result of these testimonials and considerations regarding her holiness, Hedwig was canonized by Clement IV in 1267, only twenty-four years after her death. In 1706 her feast was added to the general calendar of the Latin rite; Hedwig is honored as the patroness of Silesia.

SEVENTEEN

SAINT HEDWIG, QUEEN OF POLAND

D. 1399

THE life of St. Hedwig contains all the tragic elements that could sustain the theme of a present-day novel. The hardships she endured during her twenty-eight years of life have been carefully noted by contemporary writers and documented in the history of Poland.

Hedwig was born in 1371, the youngest of the daughters of King Louis, who was the nephew and successor to Casimir the Great. When King Louis died, he left the kingdom of Poland in a very disturbed state. Additionally, the country suffered from what amounted to a civil war over the question of who should succeed Louis to the throne since he did not have a male heir. After two years of the kingdom's instability, those who had the authority to do so agreed to accept Princess Hedwig (Jadwiga) as their sovereign. She was then only thirteen years old. She was accepted on one important condition: that the choice of her husband would meet with the authorities' approval.

According to the unanimous testimony of contemporaries, Hedwig was extraordinarily beautiful, intelligent, gentle—and above all, devout. Many were the suitors who were attracted to her attributes and her prestigious position. The attentions of these aspirants must have been very tiresome and frustrating for Hedwig, since her father had engaged her when she was four years old to William, Duke of Austria. During the nine years that followed her engagement, Hedwig had learned "to regard him as her future husband, giving him all the affection of her childish heart."

Influenced by political considerations, the Polish Diet would not approve Hedwig's marriage to William. Numerous confrontations took place between the nobles, with many continuing to plead the cause of Hedwig and William. When a final refusal was made, William disregarded all the personal dangers involved and made the romantic decision to find his promised bride and carry her off. This attempt failed; we are not told why. Hedwig could have renounced the throne in favor of her marriage to William, but given Hedwig's character it is not surprising that she sacrificed personal interests for the sake of duty.

At about this time an alliance that was politically satisfactory was presented to Hedwig as a religious duty. She was asked to marry the still-pagan Jagiello, the Grand Prince of Lithuania; he promised to become a Christian before the marriage and also pledged that all his people would receive Baptism as well. He also promised to unite his Lithuanian and Russian lands with the Polish crown and to recover at his own expense the territory which had been taken from Poland. He further promised to pay Duke William of Austria, who had been promised Hedwig's hand, an indemnity of 200,000 gulden.

Even though of tender age, Hedwig demonstrated special

maturity by acting according to her conscience. She accepted this marriage that would benefit both her country and her Church.

Nevertheless, a tremendous struggle was involved for Hedwig in agreeing to set aside William, her true love, for a loveless marriage to Jagiello, whom she did not know. This is demonstrated by the historical notation that after her decision she covered herself with a thick black veil and proceeded on foot to the cathedral of Kraków. Entering a side chapel, she fell to her knees and prayed for the next three hours for a detached heart and for perfect resignation to the will of God. She offered to Our Lord the sacrifice of her earthly happiness and all the sorrows that would purchase the salvation of so many souls. Before leaving the chapel, she spread her black veil over the crucifix to signify her sacrifice and the union of her sorrows with those of her Saviour. It is said that the crucifix is still kept and is known as the Crucifix of Hedwig.

Jagiello kept his word. He was baptized in 1383 (or 1386) and received the new name of Wladislaus. Following the marriage he was crowned King of Poland on the strength of being the consort of Queen Hedwig. Soon after the close of the coronation festivities at Kraków, a large body of ecclesiastics from Poland crossed into Lithuania, where they overcame a small resistance on the part of the heathen priests and baptized the people who gathered there in large numbers. As the result of this union between Poland and Lithuania, a mighty Christian kingdom arose in Eastern Europe, and Lithuania was for the first time brought into immediate contact with Western civilization.

During the years that followed, Hedwig governed wisely

and justly. She eliminated laws that were a hindrance to the poor and won the love of her subjects by her charity, gentleness and concern. For the newly converted people, she encouraged learning, which exerted a civilizing influence.

As for her association with Wladislaus, she seems to have exercised a moderating influence upon his headstrong and impetuous nature and to have defended herself adequately against his irrational outbursts of jealousy. We are told that she was conscientious in all her wifely duties and that her husband regarded her with deep affection. He also admired her quiet and efficient management of the kingdom and their household, as well as her spiritual qualities and her pleasant disposition.

After some time Wladislaus was overjoyed upon learning that his virtuous wife was expecting a child. He is said to have been extravagant in the preparations he made for the grand event, and he wrote from the frontier where he was conducting a campaign that he was providing jewels and rich draperies. Hedwig wrote in reply:

> Seeing that I have so long renounced the pomps of this world, it is not on that treacherous couch—to so many the bed of death—that I would willingly be surrounded by their glitter. It is not by the help of gold or gems that I hope to render myself acceptable to the Almighty Father, who has mercifully removed from me the reproach of barrenness, but rather by resignation to His will and a sense of my own nothingness.

Although wise in the administration of the kingdom and her household, Hedwig is described as having been unwise in the practice of penance, which is thought to have injured her health.

On the anniversary of her great renunciation, Hedwig went unattended to the cathedral to make a vigil before the veiled crucifix. Hours later, she was found unconscious by her ladies-in-waiting. Soon afterward the Queen went into labor and she died during childbirth. This tragedy was worsened when the baby daughter survived her mother by only a few days.

St. Hedwig was only twenty-eight years old at the time of her death in 1399. Many who had benefited from her charities and her kindness also benefited after her death by answers to prayers through her intercession and by miracles that occurred at her tomb.

EIGHTEEN

BLESSED IDA OF BOULOGNE

D. 1113

IDA is called the "Mother of Monarchs" because two of her sons, Godfrey and Baldwin, became kings of Jerusalem and her granddaughter became Queen Consort of England. Not only is her progeny titled, but her ancestors are as well, since both of her parents were descended from Charlemagne. Her father was Godfrey IV, Duke of Lorraine, and her husband was Eustace II, Count of Boulogne.

Married at the age of seventeen, Bl. Ida seems to have had a happy marriage; both husband and wife were equally dedicated to good works, especially to the restoration and building of churches. As a mother, Bl. Ida was careful in the education of her three sons, considering it her prime duty to train them in the ways of holiness and to teach them by her example all the good that can be achieved through generous almsgiving to the needy.

At the death of Count Eustace, his widow was left in control of valuable holdings. Ida had previously inherited from her father various estates in Lorraine and Germany. These holdings she arranged to sell, and the greater part of the money she derived from these sales was given to relieve the poor and in the construction of monasteries. Among the monasteries which Bl. Ida either built or restored are St. Villemar at Boulogne; St. Vaast, which accepted the religious who were sent from Cluny; the monastery of Samer; Our Lady of the Chapel, Calais; St. Bertin Abbey; and the abbeys of Bouillon and Afflighem.

Bl. Ida regarded it a blessing of the highest order that she had as her spiritual director one of the greatest men of the age, St. Anselm, abbot of Bec in Normandy, who was afterward the Archbishop of Canterbury. Some of his letters to Bl. Ida have been preserved; these indicate the generosity which she lavished on his abbey and the monies she donated for the relief of pilgrims traveling to it. In one of these letters, St. Anselm expressed his gratitude in this manner:

> You have bestowed so many and so great kindnesses upon men, whatever their order, coming to our monastery or traveling from it, that it would be wearisome to you if we were to send you messages or letters of thanks for them all; nor have we anything with which to reward you as you deserve. So we commend you to God, we make Him our agent between you and us. All that you do is done for Him; so may He reward you for us, for Him, you do so much.

Many hours were spent by Bl. Ida in praying for the success of the crusade, and it is recorded that while she was making fervent intercession for the safety of her son Godfrey, it was revealed to her that he was at that very moment making his victorious entry into Jerusalem. From him she received various relics from the Holy Land, which she distributed among several foundations.

As Ida grew older, she retired from the world. Although

she had the highest regard for monastic life, she never showed an inclination to enter a convent. She preferred to express her love for God by being a dutiful wife, a loving mother, and a generous benefactress of the poor.

Bl. Ida died when she was over seventy years old, after a long and painful illness. She was first buried in the church of the monastery of St. Vaast. The first biography of Bl. Ida was written at this monastery by a monk, a contemporary, who compared Ida to Queen Esther in the Old Testament. One chronicler suggests that Ida can also be compared to the valiant, prudent wife in Proverbs (31:10–31).

After several translations, Bl. Ida's relics finally came to rest at Bayeux.

NINETEEN

BLESSED JACOBA

D. C. 1273

LADY Jacoba di Settesoli belonged to the highest Roman nobility and was the mother of two children when she became acquainted with St. Francis of Assisi about the year 1212. When the saint was in Rome, he was often a visitor in her home, and once while visiting there he ate an excellent cream concoction called "mortairol," which is composed principally of almonds, cream, and sugar. In gratitude for Jacoba's hospitality and kindly attentions, St. Francis gave her a lamb as a gift. St. Bonaventure once claimed that the lamb seemed to have been educated by the Poverello, St. Francis, since it followed its mistress to church and remained with her while she was praying. When it was time for Jacoba's morning devotions, the lamb would awaken her by gently bumping her or bleating in her ear.

After the death of her husband, Gratian Frangipini, Jacoba was inclined to enter the religious life. However, she was prevented from doing so by the responsibility of protecting the inheritance of her two young sons, who still depended upon her care. Being unable to enter the convent, she became a member of the Franciscan Third Order.

A few days before his death, St. Francis had one of his

friars write to Jacoba to tell her, "Set out as soon as possible if you wish to see me once more. Bring with you what is necessary for my burial, and some of the good things which you gave me to eat when I was sick in Rome."

Jacoba lost little time in journeying to the hut near the Portiuncula chapel where St. Francis lay in his final illness. With her were her two sons and a great retinue, all of whom wanted to bid the saint a final farewell. Jacoba also brought with her all that was needed for the saint's burial, including a veil to cover his face, a cushion for his head, a cloth to cover his body, and all the wax candles needed for the funeral. She is also said to have brought the creamy almond dessert that he liked, but he could no more than taste it because of his condition.

When Jacoba arrived at the little hut that served as an infirmary, there was a great stir when she entered and approached the dying saint. It was strictly forbidden for women to enter the friary, but St. Francis made an exception in tender gratitude to this Roman noblewoman who had been such a special benefactress of his order. Having previously been named "Brother Jacoba" by Saint Francis on account of her fortitude, she was permitted to remain in the saint's room until his holy death.

Among Jacoba's many sufferings was the grief of witnessing the death of her two sons and of surviving her grandchildren.

Lady Jacoba apparently remained a close friend and benefactress of the Friars Minor, as verified by the insertion of her name in *The Little Flowers of St. Francis,* a book which was written a century after the death of the Poverello. Jacoba is mentioned as having visited Brother Giles in Perugia. She spent her last days at Assisi in order to be near those who knew the holy Founder.

Jacoba died about the year 1273 and is buried in the Basilica of St. Francis in Assisi. Her tomb is inscribed with the words, *Hic Requiescat Jacoba Sancta Nobilisque Romana* ("Here lies Jacoba, a noble and saintly Roman lady").

TWENTY

BLESSED JEANNE
MARIE DE MAILLE

1332–1414

A T ROCHE Ste. Quentin in Touraine, France, on April 14, 1332, a daughter was born to Baron Hardouin VI of Maille, France and his wife, Jeanne de Montbazon. The infant received the name Jeanne at her baptism, and at her confirmation that of Marie.

Jeanne Marie's father died during her adolescence, and she became the sole heir to a considerable fortune. Her grandfather, who was her guardian, judged it prudent for her to marry a young man who had been her childhood companion. He was Robert, the heir of the Baron of Sille. Although Jeanne Marie had decided to vow her virginity to God, she obeyed her grandfather and married Robert.

Previous to this, Jeanne and Robert had decided that they would live in continence. It was well-known that during their childhood they were particularly fond of each other, and at the time of their marriage there was a deep love between them. Christian virtue, order, and piety distinguished their home, which became famous as a place of relief for the poor and afflicted. While engaged in their works of charity, they came to know three orphans, whom they adopted and educated.

Their peaceful and holy situation was disturbed by war when Robert followed King John into battle in defense of his country against the English. In the disastrous Battle of Poitiers, he was seriously wounded and left for dead. When King John was captured and imprisoned, Touraine was left to the mercy of the enemy troops, who overran the land and pillaged the Chateau of Sille. Robert was imprisoned, and the sum demanded for his ransom was 3,000 florins. Since the generosity of the holy couple had drastically reduced their holdings, Jeanne Marie found it necessary to sell her jewels and horses and to borrow what was additionally needed to win her husband's freedom.

The harshness that Robert experienced during his confinement made him sensitive to the needs of prisoners, so that, upon his release, he and Jeanne Marie made many donations for the ransom of captives. They continued this and other charities while living a holy life which was characterized by self-denial until Robert died in 1362, after sixteen years of marriage.

The grief that Jeanne Marie experienced at her loss was intensified by the unkindness of Robert's family, who criticized her bitterly for impoverishing the estate through her charities. They went so far as to deny Jeanne Marie her rightful share of the estate and actually forced her from her home. With nowhere to go, Jeanne Marie took refuge with an old servant, who received her grudgingly and treated her with contempt when she learned that Jeanne Marie was without funds and was in need of charity.

Eventually Jeanne Marie journeyed to Tours, where she lived in a small house next to the Church of St. Martin. There she devoted herself to prayer, to the devotions held in the church and to the care of the poor and sick, especially lepers. She was particularly untiring in her efforts to win back to virtue women who were living an immoral life.

Having become a Franciscan tertiary, Jeanne Marie wore a distinctive dress which caused her to be insulted and mocked as she made her way on her errands of mercy. Once, a madwoman threw a stone at Jeanne Marie, which struck her back so severely that she carried the mark of the blow until her death. Not only did she suffer throughout her life from the injury caused by this blow, but to this penance she added others, including the wearing of a hairshirt.

When her husband's family restored the Chateau des Roches to her, Jeanne Marie resolved to continue a life of poverty and gave the chateau and everything else she had to the Carthusians of Liget. She also made a declaration wherein she renounced any property which might be given to her in the future. In so doing, she alienated her own relatives, who considered her a disgrace to the family.

When Jeanne Marie became completely destitute, no one would house her. She was obliged to beg from door to door and to sleep in hovels and dog kennels. For a time she worked among the servants of the hospital of St. Martin, performing the most menial chores. But there her holiness was not appreciated and she came to be humiliated, ridiculed and eventually expelled. Jeanne Marie accepted all these trials with meekness and was rewarded with visions and special graces which allowed her to understand some of the mysteries of our Faith.

When she was fifty-seven years old, Jeanne Marie began

living in a tiny room near the Minorite church at Tours. Some of the people who lived nearby considered her a madwoman or a witch, but many others recognized her as a saint.

Jeanne Marie eventually came to the attention of Louis, Duke of Anjou and Mary of Brittany, who chose her to be the godmother of their infant son. She taught the little prince about God and heaven and likewise instructed the little children in her neighborhood. These would flock around her and chant the words she had taught them, "Blessed be God and Our Lord Jesus Christ." It is said that she also taught the words to a magpie which she had tamed.

In addition to her other mystical gifts, Jeanne Marie was also given the gift of prophecy. She felt compelled to share some of the prophecies with the King, and she was once detained at court for seven days by Queen Isabel of Bavaria.

Bl. Jeanne Marie converted and healed many. She redeemed numerous men from prison and was so highly regarded by the King that he once granted her request and liberated all the prisoners in Tours.

Bl. Jeanne Marie was denied her wish to suffer martyrdom, and instead died in her poor room on March 28, 1414. She was buried in the Minorite church where she had spent so many hours in prayer.

TWENTY-ONE

BLESSED JOAN OF AZA

D. C. 1190

B L. JOAN (Jane, Joanna), the mother of the great St. Dominic, was born in the castle of Aza, near Aranda in Old Castile. Though nothing is known for certain of her childhood, it is thought that she married at an early age, according to the custom of the time and country. Her husband was Don Felix de Guzman, who was the royal warden of the small town of Calaroga in the province of Burgos. His character, we are told, rendered him in every way worthy to become her husband, and the household over which they ruled was remarkable for its piety and good order.

Bl. Joan is described as having been a person of beauty, charm, and intelligence. She was likewise pious, and she possessed great energy in the practice of good works, particularly in visiting the poor and sick in their humble dwellings. Although she was a woman of rank who had attendants to help her, she diligently applied herself to the discharge of all that was required of her state. Following the completion of her domestic duties, Bl. Joan spent the remainder of the day in prayer and frequently spent the whole night in devotional exercises.

Of this truly Christian marriage, four children were

93

born. Anthony, the eldest, became a secular priest. He was so attracted to holy poverty that he distributed his patrimony to the poor and retired to a hospital, where he spent the remainder of his days humbly ministering to the sick. Mannes, the second son, also became a priest. In due time, he became one of the first Friar Preachers and has received the honor of being beatified. A daughter was also born to the holy couple. Although her name is not given, she is known to have had at least two sons who became preaching friars.

With their two sons dedicated to the Church, Don Felix and Bl. Joan were hopeful of having another son, one who would carry on the succession of their family. For this reason Bl. Joan journeyed to the shrine of St. Dominic of Silos, a saint renowned throughout Spain for his numerous miracles. With the permission of the abbot of the monastery, Joan began a novena to the saint, spending her days and many of the nights in the monastery church absorbed in fervent prayer. On the seventh day of the novena, St. Dominic of Silos appeared to her and declared that her prayers were heard and that she would become the mother of a son who would be the light of the Church and the terror of heretics. In gratitude, Bl. Joan offered to St. Dominic of Silos the child who was to be given her through his intercession, and she promised that the child would bear the name of Dominic in honor of this favor.

Before the birth of her son, Bl. Joan beheld him in a vision, or dream; he was represented by the figure of a black and white dog holding in its mouth a torch which illuminated the whole world. This dog became a symbol of the Dominican Order and later gave rise to the pun *"Domini Canes,"* "the watchdogs of the Lord."

Sometime before Dominic's birth, Bl. Joan, in her usual generosity, distributed to the poor the entire contents of a cask of excellent wine. Realizing that her husband might become annoyed on finding the cask empty, Bl. Joan knelt down in the cellar and offered the following prayer: "O Lord Jesus, though I do not deserve to be heard, I beseech Thee, nevertheless, to take pity upon me in the name of Thy servant, and the dear little child whom I bear in my womb and whom I have consecrated to Thee." At the completion of her prayer the cask was found to be miraculously filled with wine.

At the time of Dominic's baptism, either his godmother or Bl. Joan had a vision in which there appeared on the baby's forehead a star which enlightened the whole world. Because of this vision, St. Dominic is often depicted in art with a star on his forehead.

When Dominic was only a few weeks old, Bl. Joan and Don Felix brought him to the shrine of St. Dominic of Silos and offered him to the service of God. Bl. Joan also carried the infant to the tomb of his great-uncle, Blessed Peter of Ucles, who founded the Order of the Knights of St. James of the Sword. Joan seems to have visited this place frequently; a hermitage there still bears her name.

When Dominic reached the age of seven, Bl. Joan entrusted him to the care of her brother, the archpriest of the neighboring town of Gumiel d'Izan. Another of her brothers, the abbot of La Vid, seems also to have shared in the education of the future founder of the Dominican Order.

Bl. Joan is believed to have died sometime between the years 1185 and 1194. She was buried in the parish church of Calaroga, but her remains underwent two transferals: first to the Guzman family burial place at Gumiel d'Izan; later, in 1350, to the Dominican Church at Penafiel by Prince John Emmanuel, who had a great devotion to Bl. Joan.

Butler states that it has not been given to many mothers of saints to be themselves beatified, but that Joan achieved this distinction by her own virtues and not by those of her children. He further states that the beauty of Joan's soul was shared with the greatest of her sons.

At the request of King Ferdinand VII, Joan of Aza was beatified by Pope Leo XII in 1828.

TWENTY-TWO

SAINT JULITTA AND SAINT CYRICUS

D. 304

WHEN the edicts of Diocletian were being strictly enforced against Christians, St. Julitta, a pious widow of Iconium, decided to seek safety in a more secluded location. Taking her three-year-old son Cyricus (Quiricus) and two maidservants, she went to Isauria, where she found the persecution raging under Alexander, the Governor. From there the little party traveled to Tarsus, where Julitta was promptly recognized and imprisoned.

When she was called to trial, St. Julitta appeared, leading her child by the hand. As a woman of distinction, she owned property and many possessions—but when asked about these, she answered only that she was a Christian. For her refusal to cooperate, she was condemned to be racked and scourged.

While preparations were being made to rack Julitta, the child Cyricus was taken from her. The separation caused him to cry pitifully for his mother. In an effort to comfort him, the governor took the beautiful child on his knee, but the boy would not be consoled. While his mother was being racked, he held out his arms to her and in a small voice kept repeating, "I am a Christian too." In a desperate struggle to be near his mother the child kicked Alexander and scratched his face. Furious at this behavior, the governor seized Cyricus by the foot and threw him down, fracturing his skull. The boy died almost immediately from his injury.

Overcoming her distress at seeing her child killed before her eyes, St. Julitta prayed instead of giving in to grief; she thanked God for granting her child the crown of martyrdom. The governor, still furious at the child and angry with the attitude of the mother, ordered that her sides be torn with hooks. After this was done, he ordered that she be beheaded and that her child's body should be cast out of the city with the bodies of criminals.

Following St. Julitta's execution in 304, her body and that of St. Cyricus were rescued by her two servants, who buried them in a field near the city. When peace was finally restored through the efforts of Constantine, the maids revealed the location of the graves, to the satisfaction of many Christians who came to venerate the two martyrs.

The feastday of Sts. Julitta and Cyricus was formerly observed on June 16. They are also mentioned in the calendars and menologies of the Greek and other oriental churches. Veneration of the two martyrs was common in the West at an early date, as is proved by the chapel dedicated to them in the Church of Santa Maria Antigua at Rome. In France, St. Cyricus is known as St. Cyr.

TWENTY-THREE

SAINT LEONIDAS

D. 202

AMONG the saints who died in Egypt for the Faith, one of the best-known is St. Leonidas, a learned Christian philosopher. He was a married man and the father of seven sons, of which the eldest, Origen, became known as a great Christian scholar. In fact, the fame of the son eclipsed that of his father, causing Leonidas to be sometimes identified simply as "the father of Origen." But it was due to the father that the son was able to reach such a reputation for learning, since Leonidas, aware of his child's many talents and keen intellect, gave Origen the primary education upon which his Greek literary studies depended. Leonidas likewise helped Origen in his studies of Holy Scripture. He no doubt had his son memorize what they studied together, since as an adult Origen knew the Bible so well that he could recite extended passages at will and could associate verses throughout the Bible on the basis of key words. Leonidas also provided his sons with a wholesome family life in which family prayer, the practices of their faith and the love of God held the greatest importance.

When the persecution was at its height at Alexandria, Leonidas, who was an illustrious citizen of the city, was apprehended and imprisoned on the order of Laetus, the governor of Egypt. When it seemed a certainty that his father would be martyred, Origen, then seventeen years old, was so eager to join his father in dying for the Faith that his mother locked up all his clothes to keep him at home.

While Leonidas was in prison, Origen wrote a touching letter to him, encouraging him to accept with courage and joy the crown that was offered him. Origen added, "Take heed, sir, that you do not, for our sakes, change your mind."

Leonidas stood firm in his faith and was beheaded in the year 202. The saint no doubt felt great regret at leaving his family, but we might surmise that he felt satisfied that his properties would adequately support them. The state, however, having put him to death, confiscated Leonidas' property and possessions, which reduced his wife and children to extreme poverty.

TWENTY-FOUR

SAINT LEOPOLD

1073–1136

S T. LEOPOLD III, the Margrave of Austria, was affectionately known as "Leopold the Good." He was born at Melk in 1073 and was brought up under the influence of the reforming bishop St. Altmann of Passau. When he was twenty-three years old, he succeeded his father. In 1106, when he was thirty-three years of age, he married Agnes, the daughter of Emperor Henry.

Agnes was a widow who had borne two sons by her first husband. During her marriage to Leopold, eighteen more children were added to the family. Eleven of these survived childhood. One of them was Otto, who was to become the Cistercian abbot of Marimond in Burgundy. It would be at Otto's request that St. Leopold would found the abbey of Heiligenkreuz (Holy Cross) in Wienerwald in the year 1135.

Another great foundation made by St. Leopold was Klosterneuburg, near Vienna, for Augustinian canons. Still another foundation was the Benedictine monastery of Mariazell in Styria, Austria, whose church is now a popular place of pilgrimage. By virtue of these important monasteries, Leopold did a great service to the Church, by making it possible for the true Faith to be spread throughout Austria.

Leopold's lands were twice invaded by the Magyars, but on each occasion he defeated them in the field; the second time he and his men dispatched nearly all of the enemy's forces.

When his brother-in-law Henry V died in 1125, the Bavarians wanted Leopold to claim the imperial crown, but Leopold refused to be nominated. He became a staunch adherent of Lothaire II.

After serving forty years as Margrave of Austria, St. Leopold died in 1136, at the age of sixty-three. He was buried at the Augustinian abbey of Klosterneuburg, which he had founded.

On January 6, 1485, 350 years after Leopold's death, Pope Innocent VIII proclaimed his canonization. It was the only canonization ceremony performed by this pope. Leopold was declared the national patron of Austria in 1663, with his feast being observed as a national holiday. The saint is usually pictured in a suit of armor, with a flag and a model of a church.

TWENTY-FIVE

BLESSED LOUIS OF THURINGIA

1200–1227

WHEN Louis of Thuringia was eleven years old, he was betrothed to Elizabeth of Hungary, the daughter of King Andrew II. Elizabeth at the time was four years old, and according to the custom among ruling families, the child was taken to the castle of her intended husband to be educated in the traditions and culture of her adopted land. Louis was sixteen years of age when he succeeded his father, Landgrave Hermann I. Five years later, in 1221, his marriage to Elizabeth was ratified. Louis was twenty-one years old and Elizabeth fourteen. The arranged marriage had been one of political expediency, but it proved to be also a marriage of virtuous souls and one of the happiest marriages recorded in the annals of the saints. The couple became the parents of three children, one of whom was Bl. Gertrude of Altenburg.

In his biography of St. Elizabeth, Count de Montalembert gives us a description of Bl. Louis:

> The nobility and purity of his soul were manifested in his exterior. His manly beauty was celebrated by his contemporaries. All boast of the perfect proportion of his figure, the freshness of his complexion, his long fair hair, and the serene,

benevolent expression of his countenance. Many imagined they saw in him a striking resemblance to the portrait which tradition has preserved of the Son of God made man. The charm of his smile was irresistible. His deportment was noble and dignified—the tone of his voice extremely sweet. No one could see him without loving him. What particularly distinguished him was an unstained purity of soul.

This purity was tested on two occasions, which contemporary writers have related in some detail. The first incident occurred when a certain knight wanted to put Louis' innocence to the test and found in the neighboring village a young girl of remarkable beauty. He brought her to Louis' chamber in the castle; Louis, after answering the knock at his door, was bewildered when the girl entered. When Louis asked the purpose of her visit, the knight replied that he had brought her so that Louis might do with her what he pleased. At these words Louis took the knight aside, ordered him to restore the girl to her family and warned that if any harm came to her, the knight would be hanged. The narrator of this incident stated that he concealed the name of this false knight to avoid giving scandal.

At another time Louis was standing at a window, looking down upon a square where the people were dancing. An attendant pointed out to him the wife of one of the citizens, who was remarkable for her beauty and grace. The attendant offered to make her available to Louis. Upon hearing this proposal, Louis was so shocked that he turned to the servant and said, "Be silent. If ever again thou darest to sully my ears by such language, I will drive thee from my court!"

Holy Mass was celebrated every day in the presence of

Louis and his family, and it was with exemplary devotion that he assisted. He was a zealous defender of the rights of the Church, the monasteries, and the poor. As an example of this, we are told about some Thuringian citizens who were robbed and beaten in Poland. Louis demanded reparation, but when none was forthcoming he led his troops into Poland and gained satisfaction by force of battle. The same crime then occurred at Wurtzburg. Once again Louis marched, this time to recover stock that had been stolen from a trader. It is claimed that "no sovereign of his time surpassed him in courage, nor even in physical strength and agility in the exercises of the body." He had what was called a "vehement passion for justice" and is known to have sufficiently punished violators of the law. He banished from his court those who were unkind to the poor and those who brought him false and malicious tales. Blasphemers and those who spoke "impure words" were condemned to wear a mark of shame in public. He is also known to have been cheerful and kind to his subjects and never to have offended anyone by pride or coldness.

In his association with his wife, he was most loving and thoughtful, displaying, even in the presence of others, a tenderness which was well-recorded by contemporary writers. Louis in every way approved of and encouraged the charity and devotions of his wife. Once he found in his bed a leper who had asked for relief at the door of the castle. For a moment Louis was tempted to anger, but then he saw not the leper, but the crucified Son of God. As a result of this episode, he paid for the building of a lazar house on the slope of the Wartburg.

At the request of the emperor, Louis spent several months at court assisting the emperor in restoring peace between Bologna and the cities of Lombardy. Friar Berthold tells that when Louis returned home, Elizabeth, "a thousand times and more, kissed him with her heart and with her mouth." When Louis inquired how his people had fared during his long absence, Elizabeth replied, "I gave to God what was His, and God has kept for us what was ours." To a complaining treasurer, Louis replied, "Let her do good and give to God whatever she will, so long as she leaves me Wartburg and Neuenburg."

During the following year Louis volunteered to follow Emperor Frederick II on the Sixth Crusade. He made his brother Henry regent and turned his energies to enlisting crusaders. To arouse men's hearts to this endeavor he had a Passion Play presented in the streets of Eisenach, and he visited the monasteries of his domain asking for prayers. On the Feast of St. John the Baptist, he parted from Elizabeth and set out toward the Holy Sepulchre. When the troops reached Otranto, Louis contracted the plague (or malarial fever) and became so seriously ill that the Last Sacraments were administered. The illness was to be mortal. Before Louis died it seemed to him that the cabin in which he lay was full of doves. "I must fly away with those white doves," he said, and then died. The year was 1227. He was only twenty-seven years of age. When news of his death reached Elizabeth, she cried, "The world is dead to me, and all that was pleasant in it!"

Bl. Louis' final resting place was in the Benedictine Abbey of Reinhardsbrunn, which he had often visited, and where he is popularly called "St. Ludwig."

The character and life of Bl. Louis are summed up in the noble motto which he had chosen from his earliest years: "Piety, chastity, justice towards all."

TWENTY-SIX

SAINT LUCHESIUS

D. 1260

A S A young man, Luchesius took little interest in religion; rather he was wholly occupied in worldly interests, especially money-making and politics. He made himself so unpopular by his violent partisanship of the Guelph cause in the long drawn-out dispute between the Guelph and Ghibelline parties that he found it advisable to take his family and leave Gaggiano, his native place, and to settle at Poggibonsi. There he carried on a lucrative business as a greedy merchant and grain speculator.

For some time all seemed well in the new location for Luchesius and for his wife, Buona (Bonadonna) dei Segni, and their little children. But when Luchesius was between thirty and forty years old, he underwent great sorrow when his children died. Touched by divine grace during his period of mourning, Luchesius completely changed his life. He became deeply committed to his faith, engaged in works of mercy, visited the sick, and aided prisoners. He felt that he could no longer enrich himself, as he had done in the past, by buying corn and other food items when they were cheap in order to sell them at a great profit in times of scarcity and need. His business now seemed to him to be incompatible with the lessons in Holy Scripture. To become more obser-vant of Our Lord's teachings, Luchesius and his wife gave to the poor all their possessions, except a piece of land that Luchesius wanted to cultivate by his own labor.

When St. Francis of Assisi visited Poggibonsi in the year 1221, great crowds gathered to hear his words. Among the group were Luchesius and his wife. St. Francis had either just formed his Third Order for laymen, or was in the process of forming it, when both Luchesius and his wife were accepted as members. It is a matter of dispute whether or not they were the very first members of the Franciscan Third Order. This is an organization formed for those desiring to live a spiritual life in the world under the influence of the Franciscan Order.

After becoming Franciscan tertiaries, the pious couple surrendered themselves to a most penitential and charitable life. Sometimes Luchesius would distribute to the poor every scrap of food that was in the house. Because they were already impoverished, Buona would gently speak against such extreme generosity since she was not then her husband's equal in his perfect trust in Divine Providence. But experience taught her that God supplies His faithful with all their necessities.

By virtue of his fasting, almsgiving and prayers, Luchesius attained to great sanctity and was rewarded with ecstasies, lev-itations and the gift of healing. When it became evident that he had not long to live, his wife begged him to wait a little so that she, who had shared his sufferings, might also share in his joy. Buona's prayers were answered. She died shortly before her husband; some believe they died on the same day, April 28, 1260.

St. Luchesius first gained papal attention when Gregory

X approved his cult in 1273 during a visit to Poggibonsi; Buona's cult was confirmed in 1694. A basilica that was built over the tomb of St. Luchesius about the year 1300 was almost completely destroyed by Allied bombing in 1944, but it has since been rebuilt.

TWENTY-SEVEN

SAINT LUDMILA

C. 860–921

LUDMILA was the daughter of a Slavic prince. She was also the wife of Borivoj, Duke of Bohemia. When her husband was baptized in 871 by St. Methodius, the Apostle of the Slavs, Ludmila also became a Christian. Together she and her husband built the first Christian church in Bohemia, at Levy Hradec, to the north of Prague, where Borivoj had a castle.

The two Christians met with considerable displeasure from the leading families of the area, who were opposed to Christianity. Borivoj tried to remedy the situation by forcing Christianity on his subjects, but this led to an uprising which forced him and Ludmila to seek protection in Moravia; there they remained until the leader of the rebels was assassinated.

Borivoj died when he was only thirty-five and was succeeded within a few years by his Christian sons, Sphytihnev and Ratislav. Ratislav had married a Slavic princess, Drahomira, who was a Christian in name only. When a son, Wenceslas, was born to Ratislav and Drahomira, the widowed Ludmila, then living in retirement at Prague, was entrusted with his upbringing. She was then about fifty years old, a woman of great virtue and learning.

113

It was to Ludmila's great care and instructions in the Faith that Wenceslas owed the foundation of his sanctity. Joining her in the instruction of Wenceslas was Ludmila's chaplain, Paul, who had been a disciple of St. Methodius. By the time he was ready to attend college at Budec, Wenceslas "understood Latin books as if he were a bishop and read Slavonic with ease."

The early death of the boy's father placed his mother, Drahomira, in the office of regent and made it necessary to remove Wenceslas from Ludmila's immediate charge. Drahomira sympathized with the anti-Christian party in Bohemia and was a forceful and ambitious woman. Upon learning of her son's baptism in the Christian faith and the great influence exerted over Wenceslas by Ludmila and the Catholic priest, Paul, Drahomira became exceedingly angry and envious of her mother-in-law.

Afraid that Wenceslas might seize the government before his time and promote the spread of Christianity in Bohemia, Drahomira and the anti-Christians made every effort to keep Wenceslas away from his grandmother's influence. To make certain of this, it is said that Drahomira sent two noblemen to the holy Ludmila, who strangled her with her own veil on September 15, 921.

Ludmila's body was buried in the Church of St. Michael at Tetin, but three years later, St. Wenceslas removed it with great ceremony to St. George's Church at Prague. There St. Ludmila is greatly venerated, as she is throughout Czechoslovakia.

Ludmila's death was not the only crime placed against her daughter-in-law Drahomira, since Drahomira later instigated the death of her own son Wenceslas. The murderer was Drahomira's other son, Boleslas, who hacked his brother's body to pieces.

Wenceslas is the subject of the popular Christmas carol, "Good King Wenceslas."

TWENTY-EIGHT

SAINT MACRINA THE ELDER

D. C. 340

WHEN Maximian was waging a fierce persecution against the Christians, Macrina and her husband were forced to leave their home. For a period of seven years they endured many privations while hiding in the forests of Pontus, near the Black Sea. After the danger passed, they returned to their home—but when another persecution erupted, they again suffered when their revenues, vast land-holdings, and personal possessions were confiscated. We can well imagine that St. Macrina accepted her sacrifice and loss of property with a good heart, willingly offering her privations in union with those suffered by her Saviour.

St. Macrina advanced rapidly in the spiritual life through her friendship with St. Gregory Thaumaturgus, who was the first bishop of her native town, Neocaesarea. She was the mother of at least one son, who became the father of four children who are now saints of the Church: Basil, who was later to be known as St. Basil the Great (329–379), Father and Doctor of the Church; St. Gregory of Nyssa, who was the Bishop of Nyssa and Archbishop of Sebaste, and who is also regarded as a Father of the Church; St. Peter, who also served as Bishop of Sebaste; and St. Macrina the Younger, who was the superior of one of the earliest communities of women ascetics.

It is from the writings of St. Basil that we learn something of the virtues of the saintly grandmother who implanted in the minds of these children the seeds of piety and the desire for Christian perfection which was later to raise them to the glory of sainthood. In one of his many letters, St. Basil honors and praises his grandmother in this manner:

> What clearer proof of our faith could there be than that we were brought up by our grandmother, a blessed mother, who came from among you? I have reference to the illustrious Macrina, by whom we were taught the words of the most blessed Gregory [Thaumaturgus], which, having been preserved until her time by uninterrupted tradition, she also guarded, and she formed and molded me, still a child, to the doctrines of piety.

St. Basil is apparently paying tribute to the fact that the religious instruction he received from his grandmother was so sound that he never afterward had to modify it. With reference to this he wrote:

> For, even if other matters are deserving of our groans, yet of this one thing at least I dare to boast in the Lord, that never have I held false opinions concerning God, nor did I, thinking otherwise than now, learn differently later. But the concept of God which in childhood I received from my blessed mother and from grandmother Macrina, this unfolding more completely, I have held within me, for on arriving at full reason I did not exchange one teaching for another, but confirmed those principles which they had handed over to me.

St. Macrina survived her husband, but the exact date of her death is not recorded; she is thought to have died about the year 340.

TWENTY-NINE

SAINT MARGARET CLITHEROW

(ST. MARGARET OF YORK)

1556–1586

CONSIDERED to be the first woman to have died under the religious suppression of Queen Elizabeth, Margaret was born in 1556 and lived all her life in the city of York. She was the daughter of Thomas Middleton, a wax-chandler (maker and seller of candles). He was a man of means and of some importance in the community, since he held various civic positions and for a time was a member of the Common Council. Five months after his death, his widow married Henry May, who took up residence with the family at the Middleton house in Davygate.

Margaret lived with her mother and stepfather for four years, until the age of fifteen. Then she married John Clitherow, a grazier and butcher who, as her father had been, was wealthy and held a number of civic positions. There is every indication that Margaret's early married life was happy. Three children joined the family: two boys, Henry and William, and one daughter, Anne.

Margaret had been raised a Protestant. In the manner of

girls of her class, she was taught from childhood how to run a household, but not how to read and write. Two or three years after her marriage she became a Catholic, because, as her confessor wrote of her, she "found no substance, truth nor Christian comfort in the ministers of the new church, nor in their doctrine itself, and hearing also many priests and lay people to suffer for the defense of the ancient Catholic faith." Margaret's husband did not object to his wife's conversion, but he himself remained a faithful member of the new religion of which Queen Elizabeth professed leadership.

At first, Margaret freely practiced her faith and worked toward reconciling many to the Catholic Church. She became more cautious, though, when laws against Catholics were enacted and strictly enforced. Fines were initially imposed upon Mr. Clitherow for his wife's continued absence from Protestant services; later, for her continued absence from these services, she was imprisoned in York Castle. Between the years 1577 and 1584 Margaret was imprisoned several times. The second time she was seized and imprisoned, she was released because she was expecting a child. In 1584, she was imprisoned for eighteen months.

The conditions in the prison were unbearable. Records from that time reveal that the cells were dark, damp, and infested with vermin, so that many died during their confinement. Margaret made the best of her condition by regarding her imprisonment as a time of prayerful retreat. She also used the time in learning how to read, and she returned to her home with habits of prayer and devotion which had been unfamiliar to her from her Protestant upbringing. She also began to fast four times a week, a practice she continued after her release. Her devoted husband once stated that he found but two faults in his good wife: she would not accompany him to the Protestant church, and she fasted too much.

During this time, Cardinal Allen had been conducting a seminary at Douai, France, for the purpose of training young priests who would return to their native England to minister to those who had remained loyal to the Catholic faith. When these priests returned from Douai, Catholic life began to revive in the city and the shires. Finally a law passed in 1585 made it high treason for any Englishman who was ordained a priest since the first year of Elizabeth's reign to remain in the kingdom, and it was a felony for any person to harbor or relieve a Catholic priest. By these statutes, it was only necessary to prove that a man was a Catholic priest, whether English or not, in order to condemn him to a cruel death, and a similar punishment was reserved for those who aided him.

We are not certain when Margaret began to conceal priests in her home, but when warned of the great risk she was inviting by accepting all the priests who came to her for sanctuary, she replied, "By God's grace all priests shall be more welcome to me than ever they were, and I will do what I can to set forward God's Catholic service." Margaret had in her home a secret hiding place with a passageway through which priests could hide or escape to the outside of the building. Here Frs. Thompson, Hart, Thirkill, Ingleby ,and many others took refuge. The place was apparently cramped and uncomfortable, since we are told that the entrance was "painful to him that was not acquainted with the door, by reason of the straitness thereof, and yet large enough for a boy."

Whenever a priest was visiting, Margaret arranged for the

Catholics of the area to attend Holy Mass. Fr. John Mush, her confessor and first biographer, wrote of Margaret that,

> She had prepared two chambers, the one adjoining to her own house, whereunto she might have resort any time, without sight and knowledge of any neighbours. . . . The other was a little distant from her own house, secret and unknown to any but to such as she knew to be both faithful and discreet. . . . This place she prepared for more troublesome storms, that God might yet be served there when her own house was not thought so safe, though she could not have access to it every day as she desired.

Accounts of her contemporaries reveal that Margaret was witty, happy and charming. Neighbors commented on her pleasing appearance. They noted that she spoke always in a low voice and enjoyed a simple diet of rye bread, milk, pottage, and butter. Like a true Yorkshire woman, she was careful about the neatness and cleanliness of her home, which was located in an area called The Shambles. Being a woman of some means, she had a number of servants. These she treated kindly, but she did not hesitate to correct them when their work was not properly completed. She often worked beside them to show them how to execute their chores properly.

Margaret was also a capable businesswoman, who often helped in her husband's butcher shop located near their home. She was careful that the prices she asked for her husband's wares were fair and just. "In buying and selling her wares she was very wary to have the worth of them, as her neighbors sold the like, as also to satisfy her husband, who committed all to her trust and discretion." Mindful of her husband's many responsibilities, she often urged him to close the shop with its many concerns and instead to sell only on the wholesale level, which was less troublesome.

Everyone loved Margaret, we are told. Rev. Mush recorded that her friends "would run to her for help, comfort and counsel" and he told how "with all courtesy and friendship she would relieve them." Her neighbors respected her, and even though many were of the Protestant faith, they shielded her activities and warned her of danger. Her servants, who also knew of her illegal harboring of priests, loved her and were careful to guard her secret.

She was consistent in the practice of her faith, beginning every day with an hour and a half devoted to private prayer and meditation. If a priest was available, Holy Mass followed. Margaret regularly confessed, and although she was not an educated woman, she had learned to read during her imprisonments and often read the Holy Scriptures, the works of Thomas à Kempis, and Perrin's *Exercise*. She had also learned, probably during her imprisonment, the whole of the Little Office of Our Lady.

When her son Henry came of age, Margaret obtained the permission of her husband to send him to Douai so that he might receive a Catholic education in the seminary that had been established to train missionary priests.

Sending a son or daughter outside the kingdom to receive a Catholic education was considered a crime, and as soon as the Council learned of it, John Clitherow was ordered to appear before them for questioning. Since the Clitherow house had been marked as a rendezvous for missionary priests who ministered to the Catholic inhabitants of the city, and because the authorities had learned of the Clitherows' son's absence from the kingdom, a retaliation of some sort was expected.

On March 12, 1586, while John Clitherow was testifying before the Council and Margaret was busy with her household concerns, two sheriffs of the city, accompanied by other men, entered the Clitherow house to search it. Nothing suspicious was found at first, but on opening the door to a remote room, the men found some children of the neighborhood who were being taught by a schoolmaster named Stapleton, whom they mistook for a priest. In the confusion that developed, Stapleton escaped through the secret room. Another account tells that Fr. Mush, Margaret's confessor, and Fr. Ingleby were also in the house at the time—but if so, they too escaped.

An eleven-year-old boy who was then living with the family was terrorized into revealing the secret hiding place. No one was found in the secret place, but in a nearby cupboard the authorities found church vessels, books and vestments that had been used during Holy Mass. The articles were taken as evidence and Margaret was arrested, together with all who were found in the house. The others were soon released, but Margaret was taken to the Common Hall for questioning and was then imprisoned in the castle. After being reassured that family members had been released and were safe, her good spirits returned and she promptly began to help the thirty-five women who were imprisoned with her.

During Margaret's next court appearance, the charges against her were revealed. These included the claim that she harbored and maintained priests who were working in opposition to the Queen's new religion. When the judge asked her whether or not she was guilty, Margaret replied that she had never harbored enemies of the Queen. Then, following the procedure of the court, Judge John Clinch asked her how she wished to be tried. Instead of the accepted reply, "By God and the country," Margaret replied, "Having made no offense, I need no trial." The vestments that had been found in her home during the raid were presented in evidence, but still Margaret refused to agree to a trial. Judge Clinch made every effort to get her to plead. At the same time his fellow judge, Francis Rhodes, who later had a part in the condemnation of Mary Queen of Scots, began to insult Margaret. "It is not for religion that thou harbourest priests," he called at her, "but for harlotries."

Knowing that she would die regardless of her answer, Margaret was also aware that during a trial, her children, servants, and friends would be called as witnesses and would either lie to save her and commit perjury and sin, or if they testified truthfully, would bear the burden of having caused her death. She therefore repeatedly rejected a trial and steadfastly refused to acknowledge the Protestant church of Queen Elizabeth. The Council was then forced to pronounce the sentence which English law decreed for anyone who refused to plead and be tried by a jury: *peine forte et dure,* that is, that she should be pressed to death. Margaret accepted the sentence calmly and thanked God that she would suffer for the sake of the Catholic faith.

When John Clitherow heard of the sentence passed on his wife, "He fared like a man out of his wits and wept so violently that blood gushed out of his nose in great quantity." He reportedly said, "Let them take all I have and save my wife, for she is the best wife in all England and the best Catholic, also."

Margaret was then confined in John Trew's house, where she found no peace because of the various people who visited her, trying in vain to make her acknowledge the new religion and thus gain her liberty. Even her stepfather, Henry May, who had been elected mayor of York, tried to win her over. She was not allowed to see her children and only once saw her husband, and then in the presence of a guard.

The date set for her punishment was March 25, which was also Lady Day (the Feast of the Annunciation). The evening before she was to suffer Margaret sewed her own shroud, and during the night she prayed. She had already sent her hat to her husband, "in sign of her loving duty to him as head of the family," and she had dispatched her shoes and stockings to her twelve-year-old daughter, Anne, "signifying that she should serve God and follow in her mother's steps."

At eight the next morning, March 25, 1586, female attendants helped to robe Margaret in the linen garment she had made. Surrounded by the officers of the law and by her executioners, she was then led to the place of martyrdom, only a few yards from where she had been imprisoned. To reach this place she passed through a large crowd of people who had congregated to see the strange sight of a woman led to slaughter. "All marveled to see her joyful, smiling countenance." Arriving at the place, she knelt down and with a strong voice she prayed for the pope, cardinals, clergy, Christian princes, and especially for Queen Elizabeth, that God would return her to the Faith and save her soul.

After Margaret lay down upon the ground, a sharp stone was placed under her back, and when she had extended her arms in the form of a cross, her hands were bound to posts on either side. A slab of wood the size of a door was laid over her, and weights were dropped upon it. With her bones breaking at every additional weight placed upon her, Margaret did not cry out in pain. Instead, her last words as the weight was increased were, *"Jesu, Jesu, Jesu,* have mercy upon me." Her torment lasted approximately a quarter of an hour. We are told that her body remained in the press for six hours. At the time of her death, Margaret was thirty years of age.

Margaret's crumpled body was taken by the executioners to a secret burial place. Later, when her remains were found by her Catholic friends, they were given a proper burial, although the place is now unknown. One of her hands was kept, and this is found in a crystal vessel at Bar Convent, York, which is now a museum.

The martyr's daughter, Anne, inspired by the life and death of her mother, became a nun at Louvain; her two sons, Henry and William, both became priests.

Nearly 400 years after her death, on October 25, 1970, Margaret was declared a saint by Pope Paul VI before a crowd estimated at fifty thousand in St. Peter's Basilica, Rome.

In the city of York there are many reminders of St. Margaret Clitherow. Beautifully maintained and appearing as it did in the sixteenth century is the street called The Shambles, where the Clitherow butcher shop was located. The home of the saint, at No. 35 The Shambles, is now a chapel in her honor. A service is held there every Saturday. A stone memorial is located at the place of Margaret's execution, and Catholic services are still performed in the Church of St. Martin-le-Grand, where the saint was baptized and married.

THIRTY

BLESSED MARGARET POLE

1471–1541

MARGARET Plantagenet Pole was the niece of two English kings, Edward IV and Richard III. Their brother, George Plantagenet, the Duke of Clarence, was her father; her mother was Isabel, the eldest daughter of the Earl of Warwick. Henry VII, whose wife was Margaret's cousin, gave Margaret in marriage to Sir Reginald Pole, a Buckinghampshire gentleman. The marriage, contracted in 1491, produced five children; it ended after nineteen years, in 1510, with Reginald's death. Of Margaret's five children, the fourth, Reginald, was to become Cardinal and Archbishop of Canterbury. He was also to be the indirect cause of his mother's martyrdom.

When Henry VIII ascended the throne of England, he conferred on Margaret Pole the title of Countess of Salisbury and described her as the saintliest woman in England. He also passed an Act of Restitution by which Margaret came into possession of her ancestral domains, which had been forfeited by attainder during the previous reign.

When Princess Mary was born to Henry VIII and Catherine of Aragon, the sponsor chosen for the royal infant was Margaret Pole, who was also appointed governess of the princess and head of her household. In time, Henry became attracted to Anne Boleyn, whom he wanted to marry—but first there was the matter of his marriage to Catherine. The King tried every means to have the pope annul the marriage, but when the pope refused to do this, that is, to grant an annulment, Henry himself declared the marriage invalid.

When the King married Anne Boleyn, Princess Mary was still in Margaret's care. However, Margaret was promptly removed from her post, even though she begged to remain and serve her royal charge.

After Anne Boleyn's fall, Margaret returned to court; but when her son Reginald wrote his treatise *Pro Ecclesiasticae Unitatis Defensione (In Defense of the Unity of the Church)*, which was a work against the royal claim to ecclesiastical supremacy, and refused to return to England from his self-imposed exile, Henry VIII became so incensed that he expressed the desire to rid himself of Margaret's entire family.

In November of 1538, two of Margaret's sons and others of their family were arrested on a charge of treason and were committed to the Tower. With the exception of Geoffrey Pole, they were executed in January. Ten days after the apprehension of her sons, Margaret was also arrested and was examined by Fitzwilliam, Earl of Southampton, and Goodrich, Bishop of Ely. They reported to Cromwell that although they had "travailed with her" for many hours, she would "nothing utter." They concluded that either she did not share in her sons' treason, or else she was "the most arrant traitress that ever lived." Butler comments, "They had to own that the tall, dignified woman had the brains as well as the stature of a man." She was, nevertheless, taken into custody and committed to Lord Southampton's house in Cowdray Park.

Cromwell introduced a Bill of Attainder against Bl. Margaret, and from one of her coffers he produced a white silk tunic which was embroidered on the back with intricate designs. Somehow Cromwell interpreted some of the designs as representing the Five Holy Wounds. He claimed that this connected her with Sir Henry Neville's and Bl. Thomas Percy's uprising in the North and the conspiracy connected with it, since the banner of their troops had borne symbols of the Holy Wounds. For this false charge Parliament condemned her to death without a trial. Other charges were pressed against her, to which she was never permitted to reply.

Following her conviction, Bl. Margaret was removed to the Tower where, for nearly two years, she suffered from the cold and from insufficient clothing.

On May 28, 1541, Bl. Margaret was told that she would die within the hour. Declaring that she was not guilty of the crimes lodged against her, she nevertheless walked calmly from her cell to the East Smithfield Green, within the precincts of the Tower, where a low wooden block had been prepared for her beheading. The regular executioner being absent, his understudy performed the deed and clumsily hacked at her neck. Margaret Pole was seventy years of age. Margaret was beatified in 1886, together with other English martyrs. Remembering the kindness that Henry VIII had extended to Bl. Margaret Pole at the beginning of his reign, it is ironic that she is considered to have been the first woman martyred under his Act of Supression and his persecution of Catholics.

THIRTY-ONE

SAINT MARGARET OF SCOTLAND

1045–1093

WHEN St. Edward the Confessor died without an heir to the throne of England, his nephew, Edgar Aetheling, was nominated to succeed him. Unfortunately, Edgar Aetheling was still very young and soon demonstrated his inability to defend his claim against his rival, Harold, St. Edward's brother-in-law, who seized the throne for himself.

Because Edgar Aetheling was considered the true successor, his position in England was rendered a very precarious one—and for this reason he, his mother and sisters decided to retreat to Hungary. They boarded a ship, but it met with contrary winds and was driven by storms to the Scottish coast.

There the royal family was warmly received by Scotland's King Malcolm III. By this hospitality Malcolm returned the favor which England had afforded him years earlier, following the murder of Malcolm's father, King Duncan. At that time, Malcolm had been forced to leave Scotland and had taken refuge in England. Edward the Confessor had then afforded him every courtesy, even helping him to regain his kingdom.

While Edgar Aetheling, together with his mother and his sisters, were in the Scottish court, King Malcolm—a widower—became captivated by the charms of Edgar's sister, Princess Margaret, who was as beautiful as she was accomplished. Although her natural inclination would have led her to prefer the cloister, Margaret realized that her duty lay elsewhere; she yielded to the wishes of her mother and the Scottish king.

Margaret's wedding to King Malcolm, which was celebrated amid national rejoicing, took place at the Castle of Dunfermline in the year 1070, when Margaret was twenty-five years old. The marriage was to bring great blessings upon Malcolm and Scotland. Largely because of Margaret's virtues, the union proved to be a very happy one.

Soon after the wedding, Margaret's mother and sister returned to England, where they entered religious life, one at Winchester and the other at Romsey Abbey in Hampshire. They left Margaret in a foreign land with a husband who was rough, uncultured, could neither read nor write, and who, as a warrior, had led raids in England, dragging into captivity multitudes of fair-haired Saxons. But, in spite of all his faults, Malcolm had a willingness to amend his shortcomings and a great desire to please his new bride. Through the great influence she acquired over him, Margaret softened his temper, polished his manners, and rendered him one of the most virtuous kings who has ever occupied the Scottish throne. Soon the couple's chief objective in life became to maintain justice, make their subjects happy and establish religion. One of the saint's early biographers wrote, "She incited the King to works of justice, mercy, charity and other virtues, in all which by divine grace she induced him to carry out her pious wishes. For he, perceiving that Christ dwelt in the heart of his queen, was always ready to follow her advice."

The change which Margaret produced in her husband was extended to her adopted country. She promoted civilization and encouraged education for her subjects. She criticized the long delays in the courts of justice, and she asked that the suits of the poor be given preference over those of others. She urged her husband to correct his soldiers and to forbid them to pillage the homes of the Scottish people. She settled quarrels and ransomed many of the Saxon slaves whom Malcolm had brought to Scotland.

Marriage laws, as well as the observance of Lent and Easter, were regulated, and trading on Sundays was rendered unlawful—although this reform met with stubborn resistance. Margaret defended her case with arguments taken from Holy Scripture, and she was so convincing in doing so that all opposition ceased. Margaret also stressed that thanksgiving to God should be given after every meal—a prayer that became known as St. Margaret's Blessing. With her husband, St. Margaret founded several churches, notably that of the Holy Trinity at Dunfermline.

To correct many grave abuses among priests and the people, she instigated synods, whose rules were helpful in correcting various evils. Perhaps St. Margaret's principal success lay in bringing the Church in Scotland into union with the Roman Church. She made it her constant effort to obtain priests who were eminent for their learning and virtue, and she implored her husband to give them positions of influence.

Margaret's confessor, Bishop Turgot, wrote a beautiful biography of the saint in which he gave an inspiring picture of the influence she exercised over the rude Scottish court.

Among the ladies of the court, St. Margaret formed an embroidery guild to provide vestments and altar linens. In referring to the guild and the care, St. Margaret took to regulate the behavior of the ladies while they were performing a service for the Church, Bishop Turgot wrote:

> These works were entrusted to certain women of noble birth and approved gravity of manners who were thought worthy of a part in the Queen's service. No men were admitted among them, with the sole exception of such as she permitted to enter along with herself when she paid the women an occasional visit. There was no giddy pertness among them, no light familiarity between them and the men; for the Queen united so much strictness with her sweetness of temper, so pleasant was she even in her severity, that all who waited upon her, men as well as women, loved her while they feared her, and in fearing loved her.

Bishop Turgot goes on to describe Margaret's disposition and holy conduct:

> While she was present no one ventured to utter even an unseemly word, much less to do aught that was objectionable. There was a gravity in her very joy, and something stately in her anger. With her, mirth never expressed itself in fits of laughter, nor did displeasure kindle into fury. Sometimes she chided the faults of others—her own always—with that commendable severity tempered with justice which the Psalmist directs us unceasingly to employ, when he says, "Be ye angry and sin not." Every action of her life was regulated by the balance of the nicest discretion, which impressed its own distinctive character upon each single virtue. When she spoke, her conversation was seasoned with the salt of wisdom; when she was silent, her silence was filled with good thoughts. So thoroughly did her outward bearing correspond with the staidness of her character that it seemed as if she had been

born the pattern of a virtuous life. I may say, in short, every word that she uttered, every act that she performed, showed that she was meditating on the things of heaven.

Margaret's private life was most austere: she ate sparingly, and in order to obtain time for her devotions she permitted herself only a minimum amount of sleep. Every year she kept two Lents: the one at the usual season, and the other before Christmas. During these penitential times she always rose at midnight and went to church for Matins. The king often shared her vigils. She also had scheduled times during the day for prayer and spiritual reading. We are told that although Malcolm could not read, he loved to handle his wife's books of devotion and would often take them secretly to have them illuminated or ornamented with gold and precious stones. One of the most prized of these books was a copy of the Gospels which the Queen took with her on her travels. On one occasion it was accidently dropped by a servant into a stream which they were crossing. When it was finally removed from the water, the book was found unharmed except for a small watermark on the cover. The book is now preserved among the treasures of the Bodleian Library at Oxford.

Perhaps St. Margaret's most outstanding virtue was her love of the poor. She often visited hospitals, in which she tended the patients with her own hands. She erected hostels for strangers and ransomed many captives, especially those of English nationality. When she appeared outside her palace she invariably was surrounded by beggars, none of whom went away unaided.

The royal couple was blessed with eight children; six sons:

Edward, Edmund, Edgar, Ethelred, Alexander, and David; and two daughters: Matilda (Maud) and Mary. With the utmost care, Margaret instructed them in the Christian faith and supervised their other studies. When the princesses were old enough, Margaret made them the companions of her spiritual exercises and works of mercy.

Matilda married Henry I of England and came to be known universally as the Good Queen Maud. On her tomb was written in golden letters, "A day would not suffice to tell of all her goodness and uprightness of character." Mary became the wife of Count Eustace of Boulogne and the mother of Matilda, who gave birth to Stephen, the English king. Three sons, Edgar, Alexander and David, successively occupied the Scottish throne and proved capable and pious rulers; in fact, David reigned for twenty-nine years and is commonly regarded as one of the best and noblest of the Scottish kings. Ethelred became the Abbot of Dunkeld and Earl of Fife. Edmund, after a careless and wandering life, repented and became a monk. The eldest son, Edward, joined his father in the following ill-fated expedition.

In the year 1093, William Rufus, who had succeeded to the English throne, surprised and captured Alnwick Castle. King Malcolm demanded restitution of the fortress, which had previously belonged to Scotland; and when it was refused, he laid siege to the castle. The English defenders, after suffering greatly from the situation, offered to surrender if Malcolm would come in person to receive the keys. Malcolm rode out to meet them. He leaned forward to accept the keys, which were presented to him on the point of a spear. As his fingers were about to touch the keys, the soldier who was holding the spear thrust the weapon through the King's eye, killing him.

Margaret's son, Edward, carried on the siege to avenge his father, but advanced too recklessly and was slain as well. With both leaders dead, the Scots abandoned the siege and relinquished rights to the castle.

During the last six months of her life, St. Margaret was confined to her bed. The day her husband was killed she seemed exceptionally sad and restless, and she said to her attendants, "Perhaps this day a greater evil hath befallen Scotland than any this long time." When her son Edgar arrived back from Alnwick, she asked how his father and brother were. Afraid that the sad news might weaken his mother, he replied that they were well. She looked at him and exclaimed, "I know how it is!" Then raising her hands toward heaven she said, "I thank Thee, Almighty God, that in sending me so great an affliction in the last hour of my life, Thou wouldst purify me from my sins, as I hope, by Thy mercy."

On November 16, 1093, St. Margaret died. This took place four days after her husband's death, when she was forty-seven years of age. She was buried at Dunfermline before the high altar, where years earlier she had become the bride of the Scottish king. The Abbey Church of Dunfermline was largely destroyed in 1560 by the Protestant reformers.

St. Margaret was canonized by Pope Innocent IV in 1250. Her feast is observed on November 16, the anniversary of her death.

THIRTY-TWO

SAINT MATILDA

895–968

A T A time when it was customary for girls of gentle birth to be educated in convents, Matilda was confided to the care of her paternal grandmother, the abbess of the convent of Erfurt. Born about the year 895, Matilda was the daughter of Dietrich, a powerful Westphalian count and Reinhild of the royal Danish house. When Matilda reached womanhood, news of her beauty, piety and learning reached Duke Otto of Saxony; he was seeking a suitable wife for his son, Henry, who had recently obtained an annulment of his marriage to a woman named Hathburg. Following the dissolution of their marriage, Hathburg retired into a convent. It was only then that Henry journeyed to Erfurt to win the hand of the beautiful Matilda.

It is said that Henry fell in love with Matilda at first sight. She was sitting in the oratory, psalter in hand and absorbed in devotion when Henry first saw her. It is speculated that Matilda was as captivated by the charms of her admirer as he was of her. Henry was then thirty-three years old. He was tall, handsome, and had "flashing and penetrating eyes . . . he was joyous in festivities, but without diminishing his dignity. In war he was loved and feared." Henry is said to have been "overmuch addicted to hunting," and engaged too often in hawking, a sport which was then very popular. This sport won for him the nickname of "the Fowler," a name that followed him through history.

The marriage was celebrated with great festivities in 909 at Wellhausen. The union was well-received and proved to be an exceptionally happy one, Matilda bringing to her husband a wholesome, virtuous influence. Three years after their wedding, Matilda gave birth to her first son, Otto, and soon thereafter Henry succeeded to his father's dukedom. Then, at the beginning of the year 919, when King Conrad died without an heir, Henry was raised to the German throne. In this capacity it became necessary for him to lead his soldiers into warfare. Matilda feared for her husband's safety while he fought with great success against the Danes, the Bohemians, the Hungarians, and other aggressors.

While Henry was victorious in these endeavors, part of his success was attributed to the prayers of Matilda, who was known as an exceptionally good and pious queen. It is said that throughout her life she retained the humility which had distinguished her as a girl and that she lived a simple life, although surrounded by the trappings of the royal palace. To her servants she seemed a loving mother; to the distressed, someone who always relieved their sufferings; to her subjects she lightened their burden of taxation and increased their prosperity. If Matilda was a generous queen and a loving wife and mother, Henry was a benevolent king and a thoughtful and kind husband. Together with her husband, Matilda planned good and just laws and worked hard for the advancement of the Church. Although his wife was liberal in almsgiving, Henry never complained, nor did he show irritation at her pious practices. He trusted her in all things and depended upon her good advice and prayers.

Their happy marriage was blessed with five children: Otto, who became the Emperor of the Holy Roman Empire; Henry the Quarrelsome, who became the Duke of Bavaria; St. Bruno, who became Archbishop of Cologne; Gerberga, who married Louis IV, King of France; and Hedwig, who became the mother of Hugh Capet.

When King Henry suffered a serious apoplectic seizure, Matilda rushed to church to pray for his recovery; but while she was at the foot of the altar, word was brought of Henry's death. She at once arranged for a priest to offer Holy Mass for the repose of his soul and, in the fullness of her grief, she removed the jewels she was wearing and gave them to the priest as a pledge that she renounced, from that moment onward, all the pleasures of the world. The holy couple had been married for twenty-three years.

King Henry had expressed a wish that his eldest son, Otto, should succeed him, but Matilda favored her son Henry, and persuaded a few nobles to vote for him. In the end, Otto was chosen and crowned. Matilda is said to have "expiated her unjust partiality by severe afflictions and in the end by voluntary penance." The matter, however, did not end with Otto's coronation, since his brother, Henry, unwilling to give up his claim, raised a rebellion against him. After Henry discovered that he could not win, Otto pardoned him and made him Duke of Bavaria.

Matilda continued living in the palace, but her life was

one of penance, prayer, and works of charity. She wore the simplest clothes and was frugal in her food and drink. All her jewelry was given over for the benefit of the poor, and her generosity was such as even to arouse criticism. Her son Otto finally accused her of having a secret treasury and of wasting the crown revenues. He forced upon his mother the indignity of having her give an accounting of all she spent, and he even sent spies to watch her movements and to check the amount of her donations. As if this were not enough of a humiliation, she was sorrowed upon learning that her favorite son, Henry, was aiding and siding with his brother against her. With humility and patience she bore her trial, once remarking with what is called "a touch of pathetic humor" that it was a consolation to know that her sons were united, even though it was only to persecute her.

To satisfy them, Matilda resigned the inheritance and gave up the properties left her by her husband and retired to the country residence where she had been born. But as soon as she left, Duke Henry became ill and one misfortune after another fell upon the Kingdom. Since it was felt that this was a punishment for the treatment given the Queen by her sons, Otto's wife, Edith, persuaded her husband to recall his mother, to ask her forgiveness and to restore all he had taken from her. Matilda freely forgave her sons and returned to court, where she resumed her charities. These included nursing the sick, feeding the hungry, bathing those whose afflictions prevented them from doing this for themselves, and paying the fines of those who were imprisoned for debt.

St. Matilda had fires lighted in public places to relieve the sufferings of the homeless during the winter months, and she distributed lanterns so that they would not lose their way in the dark.

The trials St. Matilda suffered because of the disagreements of her two sons once again fell to her when the unhappy Henry began another revolt against Otto. Afterwards, he punished a rebellion in his own Bavaria with incredible cruelty, sparing not even the clergy. It seems that the nickname "the Quarrelsome" was appropriately annexed to his name by historians. St. Matilda was deeply saddened by his conduct, and when in 955 she saw him for the last time she prophesied his approaching death and pleaded with him to be reconciled with the Church. When the news of his death reached her, she was prostrated with grief. In his memory, she established a number of convents and monasteries.

Otto apparently reconciled completely with his mother and showed his leniency with her charitable activities by leaving the kingdom in her charge while he journeyed to Rome to be crowned Emperor of the Holy Roman Empire.

Matilda had the pleasure of a family reunion at Cologne on Easter of 965. With all her surviving children around her she was treated with an outpouring of love and honor. It was her great consolation that one of her sons, Bruno, became a priest and afterward Archbishop of Cologne. Following this gathering of the family, Matilda retired from the world, spending her time in visiting her foundations.

At Quedlinburg, she contracted a fever which developed into a terminal situation. Realizing that her death was approaching, she sent for Richburga, the abbess of Nordhausen, who had formerly been her lady-in-waiting and had assisted her in all her charities. According to the traditional story, the Queen proceeded to give away everything in her room until she was told that only her burial linen remained. She instructed them to give it to her grandson, Bishop William of Mainz, who died very suddenly twelve days before his grandmother's death.

The saint died a most humble death in the year 968 after receiving the Last Rites. Her body was buried beside that of her husband in the church of the Convent of St. Servatius and Dionysius at Quedlinburg, East Germany. Matilda was regarded as a saint immediately after her death.

THIRTY-THREE

SAINT MONICA

331–387

S T. MONICA was born of Christian parents in North Africa, probably at Tagaste, sixty miles from Carthage. Her early training was entrusted to a faithful retainer who had been a nurse to other young members of the family, including Monica's father. This servant was wise in her treatment of her young charge, but somewhat strict. One of her regulations was that of never drinking between meals. This led to one of the few incidents recorded of Monica's early life. What we know of this and other details of her life were given to us by her son, St. Augustine, in his *Confessions*. In Book IX, Chapter VIII, he tells that the servant strictly enforced this regulation, "preventing thereby a naughty custom." St. Augustine records the servant as having said, "Now ye drink water because ye are not suffered to have wine; but when once you come to be married, and be made mistress of butteries and cellars, you will scorn water then, but the custom of drinking will prevail upon you."

By virtue of this teaching the servant "brought the girl's thirst to so honest a moderation, as that now they cared not for what was not comely."

But, as St. Augustine relates:

There stole upon her a lickerish inclination toward wine. For when, as the manner was, she, being thought to be a sober maiden, was bidden by her parents sometimes to draw wine out of the hogshead, she, holding the pot under the tap, would at the mouth of it, before she poured the wine into the flagon, wet her lips as it were with a little sip of it. . . . And thus unto that daily little every day adding a little more (for whoever contemneth small things, fall by little and little), fell she at last to get such a custom, that she would greedily take off her cups brimful almost of wine.

St. Augustine relates that his mother's attraction for wine was checked by a servant who, in a physical manner, made the future saint realize the seriousness of her actions.

For a maid which she used to go withal into the cellar, falling to words, as it happened, hand to hand with her little mistress, hit her in the teeth in a most bitter insulting manner, calling her "wine-bibber" with which taunt she being struck to the quick, reflected upon the foulness of her fault, yea, and instantly condemned it to herself, leaving it quite.

Following this confrontation with her maid, Monica never again gave way to temptation, and following her baptism, which occurred soon afterward, she lived an exemplary life in every detail.

As soon as she reached a suitable age, her parents gave her in marriage to Patricius, a pagan and a citizen of Tagaste. Unfortunately, Patricius was violent-tempered and dissolute. St. Augustine tells us, "She so discreetly endured his wronging of her bed, that she never had any jealous quarrel with her husband for that matter. Because she still expected Thy mercy upon him, that believing in Thee, he might turn chaster."

St. Augustine describes his father as being "of a passing

good nature, also very hot and irritable." Patricius never physically abused his wife, although it seemed the custom for the women of that area to have on their bodies and faces the bruises of their domestic difficulties. They were amazed that Monica never displayed signs of ill-treatment from a husband whom they knew was difficult and verbally abusive. One day Monica confided to the women her method of handling an annoyed husband: "Guard your tongue when your husband is angry." St. Augustine says, "Those wives that observed it, finding the good, gave her thanks for it; those that did not were kept under and afflicted."

In addition to having a difficult husband, Monica also had a difficult mother-in-law whose presence, as a permanent resident of the house, added considerably to the younger woman's difficulties. Afterward, when the mother-in-law came to realize that it was the gossiping of the servants that sparked her dislike of Monica, she had the servants severely reprimanded. In addition, she promised a harsh punishment for anyone who would again speak against her daughter-in-law. St. Augustine adds, "They lived ever after with a most memorable sweetness of mutual courtesies."

Patricius and Monica had at least three surviving children: a daughter, Perpetua; a son, Navigius, who was to be his mother's support during many difficulties; and Augustine (354–430), whose love of pleasure and carefree attitude was to cause his mother many years of anxiety.

During their years of marriage, Monica's goodness influenced her husband to learn more of the true Faith. He was eventually enrolled among the catechumens and later was baptized. Thereafter, the relationship of the couple developed into a warm spiritual devotion, which was heightened by their mutual love of the Church. Only one year after his baptism, Patricius became ill and suffered acutely for several months. With Monica in devoted attendance, she attempted by every means to alleviate his pain. He died in the peace and joy of his faith, with his saintly wife beside him.

At the time of his father's death, Augustine was a seventeen-year-old catechumen, awaiting baptism. He was also a student in Carthage, devoting himself especially to rhetoric. Monica was soon to learn, to her great unhappiness, that Augustine was indulging in all the vices of a carefree and self-indulgent young man. Although Monica pleaded with him to abandon his sinful life, Augustine ignored her efforts. While studying science and philosophy, he joined a group that prided itself with being against the established order. During this time he became infatuated with a young woman, and for the next fifteen years he lived with her in an unmarried state. She gave birth to a son, who was named Adeodatus. Sometime during these fifteen years, he publicly renounced the Catholic faith and declared that he was aligned with the Manichaean heresy. Once when Augustine attempted to visit his mother, Monica forcibly demonstrated her displeasure with her son's activities by refusing to let him stay in her house or eat at her table.

A prophetic vision was given Monica about this time. She seemed to be standing on a wooden beam, while weeping over her son's sinful life, when a celestial being inquired about the cause of her grief. He then told her to dry her eyes, adding, "Your son is with you." Looking toward the spot he indicated, she saw Augustine standing on the beam beside her.

When she told Augustine about the dream, he sarcastically remarked that they might easily be together if Monica would reject her faith. She promptly replied, "He did not say that I was with you; he said you were with me." Monica's ready reply made a deep impression upon her son. This occurred about the end of the year 377, almost nine years before Augustine's conversion.

Monica prayed and fasted to effect her son's conversion. Once, while asking the advice of a wise bishop who had formerly been a Manichaean himself, he reassured her with words that have since become famous: "Go now, it is not possible that the son of so many tears should perish."

When Augustine was twenty-nine years old and planned on teaching rhetoric in Rome, Monica opposed the plan, thinking that this would delay his conversion. On learning that his mother intended to accompany him, he deceived her into thinking that he was going to the docks to bid farewell to a friend, whereas he actually set sail without notifying her. Although grieved at this trickery, she followed Augustine to Rome only to learn that he had continued on to Milan. There he came under the influence of the great bishop St. Ambrose. By the time Monica finally joined her son she was greeted with the pleasant news that he was no longer a Manichaean, although not yet a baptized Catholic. To St. Ambrose she expressed heartfelt gratitude. The holy bishop, for his part, had the highest opinion of St. Monica and never tired of praising her to her son.

For some time, Monica had been trying to arrange a suitable marriage for her son; but in August of 386, Augustine told her what she had been waiting and praying for—that he completely accepted the Catholic faith. Moreover, he declared that he would, from then on, live a celibate life. Before Augustine's baptism, Monica joined him and his friends in pious conversations, some of which are recorded in the *Confessions*. During these discussions, Monica displayed remarkable insight and judgment and showed herself to be exceptionally well-versed in the Holy Scriptures. At Easter in the year 387, St. Ambrose baptized St. Augustine and some of his friends.

On its way back to Africa during the same year, the group reached Ostia, where it became necessary for them to await the arrival of their ship. During their stay, Monica contracted her final illness. Before she died she expressed her appreciation to Almighty God for having fulfilled all her hopes. The greatest of these were Augustine's conversion and consecration into the service of the Church. On being asked if she would not be afraid to die and be buried so far from home, the saint replied, "Nothing is far from God, neither am I afraid that God will not find my body to raise it with the rest." After a five-day coma, Monica regained consciousness and said to her sons, "Here you will bury your mother." Navigius expressed the hope that she would recover and return home with them, but she repeated her request and added, "The one thing that I ask of you both is that you should remember me at the altar of the Lord, wherever you may happen to be." After an agony of several days, Monica died peacefully. St. Augustine records that the saint died in the "six and fiftieth year of her age, and the three and thirtieth of mine."

Augustine considered it unbecoming to cry at the funeral of one who had died a holy death, but when he was alone he wept bitterly while considering what she had endured for his sake. His love for his mother and the bitter grief he experienced at her passing are recorded at length in his *Confessions.*

St. Monica was first buried at Ostia, but her relics are now kept in the Church of St. Augustine in Rome. They can be found under the altar of the Blessed Sacrament at the end of the left aisle.

St. Augustine went on to become the Bishop of Hippo. By virtue of his strong and lasting influence on Christian theology and philosophy, he is now recognized as a Doctor of the Church.

Successive generations of the faithful have venerated St. Monica as a special patroness of married women, and a pattern for all Christian mothers, especially mothers of wayward children. Having prayed for St. Augustine's conversion for seventeen years, she is a worthy example and a source of encouragement for mothers who might at times become discouraged by the resistance of their children to reform their lives. These mothers may take courage in the fact that, in praying so diligently for her son, this mother not only produced a saint for the Church, but in the process also attained sainthood herself.

St. Monica's feast day is observed on August 27; St. Augustine's is celebrated the following day, August 28.

THIRTY-FOUR

SAINT NICHOLAS
OF FLÜE

1417–1487

ALTHOUGH he is not recognized as the patron saint of Switzerland, St. Nicholas occupies a unique place with his countrymen and is perhaps Switzerland's best-known religious figure. His history is interesting in that, during his lifetime, he was a farmer, soldier, magistrate, judge, councillor, father of ten children, and a hermit.

Nicholas was born in 1417 of a relatively wealthy and much respected farming family. His father was Henry von Hite, who held a civil post in the cantonal service, in addition to his farming duties. Nicholas' mother, Emma Robert, was a devout woman whose two sons, Nicholas and Peter, joined her in a religious organization known as *Gottesfreunde,* or Friends of God. The members of this society tried, by a life of strictness and devotions, to adhere loyally to the practices of the Catholic Church, with an aim at a close relationship with God. Nicholas was especially responsive to his mother's good example and the training he received; he was remarkable from childhood for his piety, his love of peace, and his sound judgment.

At the age of twenty-two, this peace-loving man was

drafted into the army and fought in the war with Zurich. A fellow soldier recorded that Nicholas "did but little harm to the enemy, but rather always went to one side, prayed, and protected the defeated enemy as best he could."

Sometime after this campaign, Nicholas married a religious-minded girl named Dorothea Wissling, with whom he lived happily; but in 1460, he was again drafted into the army during the Thurgau War. This time he was the captain of a company consisting of 100 men. In this responsible position he maintained strict discipline, restraining his soldiers from all excesses, and succeeded in saving the Dominican convent of St. Catherine at Diesenhofen, which others wanted to burn because it was suspected of being a refuge of the enemy.

Upon his return from the war, Nicholas' countrymen appointed him magistrate and judge and sent him to councils and meetings where his clear-sighted wisdom was highly respected. By his own admission, he had considerable authority as a judge and councillor, but he also said that he did not remember ever having been unjust or having acted in consideration of a person's social position. Despite his obvious talents, he despised temporal honors and repeatedly refused the highest post of all, that of landamman, or governor. A contemporary has said of him:

> A noble simplicity ruled his speech. He displayed such balance of judgment in the cases brought before him that his decision immediately convinced everyone as being right. His spirit of justice and impartiality, as well as his reputation for piety and mercy, had gained for him widespread confidence, and he was often chosen arbiter in serious controversies.

Another contemporary has said, "He was a friend of peace, a defender of widows and orphans; he was merciful and exhorted the others to show mercy."

Throughout the years of his married life, the holy man continued the devout practices of his youth, and his ten children were all educated in the Faith. The youngest son, Nicholas, developed a vocation to the priesthood and studied at the University of Bale, where he earned a doctorate degree in theology. For many years he served as the parish priest of Sachseln. John, the eldest son, became landamman during his father's lifetime; he testified to his father's virtue as follows: "My father always retired to rest at the same time as his children and servants; but every night I saw him rise again and heard him praying in his chamber until morning. Often, too, he would go in the silence of the night to the old church of St. Nicholas or to other holy places."

At times Nicholas would also retire into solitude in the valley of the Melch, but when he was about fifty years old he felt irresistibly drawn to abandon the world altogether and to spend his days in the contemplative life of a solitary. He revealed this new vocation to his wife, who recognized the will of God and did not oppose her husband. Nicholas resigned his offices, placed his affairs in order and took leave of his wife, his father, and all his children on October 16, 1467, just three and a half months after the birth of his last child. Nicholas must have amply provided for his family's financial future, because the family never seems to have suffered in a material fashion from the loss of its provider.

At the time of his leaving, Nicholas went barefoot and bareheaded, wearing simple clothes and carrying in his hands his rosary and his staff. His destination appears to have been Strasbourg, but before crossing the frontier, he received the hospitality of a peasant, a Friend of God, who persuaded him to remain in his own country. The next morning, when a fierce thunderstorm produced lightning in the direction in which he meant to travel, Nicholas accepted this as a sign from God and retraced his steps.

It is recorded that one evening during the homeward journey, as he lay under a tree, Nicholas was seized with such violent gastric spasms that he thought his last hour had come. The pain passed, but from that time on he lost all desire for ordinary food or drink and maintained a perpetual fast. According to his own description of what took place, he said that, "A light from heaven seemed to surround me, and I felt in my intestines a violent pain, as if someone had first probed them with a sharp knife and then cut them out. From that instant, I have never felt the need of human food or drink, and have never used them."

Months later, hunters discovered Nicholas in a pasture, where he had made himself a shelter of boughs and moss. When word was brought to his brother Peter and his friends, they went to caution him that he might die of exposure. They successfully persuaded Nicholas to move to Ranft, another part of the valley, where the people of Obwalden built him a little cell with an attached chapel.

In this place, Nicholas spent nineteen peaceful years. His days were carefully planned, with the morning hours being spent in prayer. Having received from God the gift of counsel, Nicholas spent the afternoon and evening hours interviewing pilgrims, churchmen, and politicians who came to ask for his advice on spiritual or temporal matters. His perpetual fast attracted many of the curious, who were given the reply, "God knows" when they asked about it. The truth concerning his perpetual fast was verified by the cantonal magistrates, the physician of Archduke Sigismund and envoys of Emperor Frederick III. Once a year, Nicholas took part in the great procession in Lucerne, but otherwise he only left his retreat to attend divine service in a nearby church, and he occasionally visited the Blessed Mother's shrine at Einsiedeln.

The faithful added a room to Nicholas' chapel in his later years. This room served as the residence of a priest, who offered daily Mass for the saint. The wife and children of Nicholas frequently attended Mass here and were at times among the pilgrims who listened to his words of spiritual counsel. When the need arose, his wife and children did not hesitate to ask his advice in their personal difficulties or concerning the affairs of the household.

When the cantons came together at the Diet of Stans to negotiate a settlement of their opposing positions, which threatened a civil war, their fierce arguments obstructed a resolution of the matter. When they were at the point of returning home to settle matters by arms, the parish priest of Stans stood up and suggested that they should ask the opinion of Blessed Nicholas on how best to settle their differences. The cantons gave their consent, and sent the priest and perhaps others to the cell of the holy man. Some have suggested that the charter known as the Edict of Stans was drafted in the presence of Nicholas at his retreat, while the chronicler Diebold Schilling tells that the priest Imgrund arrived back in Stans to relay the solution given him by Nicholas. Schilling does not record the words of the message, but he informs us that within an hour, the council had arrived at a unanimous agreement. The date was December 22, 1481.

That Christmas, with a war averted, the whole of Switzerland celebrated joyously, and the Stans Council expressed, in laudatory terms, its gratitude to Nicholas for his wise recommendations. Letters of thanks from Berne and Soleure to the holy man are still extant, as well as a letter written on his behalf by his son John, thanking Berne for a gift of money which would be expended upon the Church.

One of the saint's visitors, Albert von Vonstetten, dean of the monastery of Einsiedeln, gives us a description of the saint. He was described as being tall, brown and wrinkled, with thin grizzled locks, a short beard, bright eyes, white teeth, and a shapely nose. The dean adds, "He praises and recommends obedience and peace. As he exhorted the Confederates to maintain peace, so does he exhort all who come to him to do the same."

Six years after the Council of Stans, Nicholas was seized with his last illness, which lasted eight days and caused him extreme suffering. He bore his affliction with perfect resignation and died peacefully in his cell, on his birthday, having reached the age of seventy. Immediately after his death he was honored in all Switzerland as a patriot and as a saint, but his cultus was not formally sanctioned until 1669.

His remains are found in a shrine under a black marble canopied altar of the present church of Sachseln. The clothes formerly worn by the saint are said to be kept in a cupboard of the church, but his rosary was broken in pieces for distribution among members of his family.

162

In 1917, the fifth centenary of the birth of "Bruder Klaus" was celebrated throughout Switzerland with remarkable enthusiasm. Thirty years later, his name was added to the list of saints, when he was canonized in 1947 by Pope Pius XII.

THIRTY-FIVE

SAINT NONNA

D. 374

NONNA was raised a Christian, but she married Gregory, the Magistrate of Nazianzus, who was a member of a sect called the Hypsistarians. This "mixed marriage" eventually resulted in the conversion of the husband, and the birth of three children, all of whom are saints of the Church. St. Nonna is credited with producing for the Church one of the most famous, brilliant and saintly families of Christian history. The eldest child was St. Gregory of Nazianzus the Divine, who served as the Bishop of Nazianzus and became one of the greatest of the Doctors of the Church. His funeral orations for his sister, brother, father, and mother are extant and give us wonderful details concerning the virtuous life of his family. The next child was St. Gorgonia, who married and had three children. The third was St. Caesarius, a physician by profession who chose to live in virtuous poverty while tending the ailments of the poor.

St. Nonna suffered the pangs of grief in witnessing the death of two of her children. Gorgonia died in her arms, and she heard the eulogy preached for her son, Caesarius, by her eldest son, St. Gregory of Nazianzus. In this eulogy, St. Gregory gave credit to his holy parents for the many virtues of his brother and praised his parents in this way:

> This good shepherd [his father] was the product of his wife's prayers and guidance, and it was she who taught him the ideal of a good shepherd's conduct. He nobly fled from his idols, and later put demons to flight. . . . They have been one in honor, one in mind, one in soul, and their bond no less a union of virtue and intimacy with God than of the flesh. They are equal in length of life and gray hairs, equal in prudence and splendor . . . they have despised this world and preferred the world beyond. They have cast aside riches, yet they abound in riches through their noble traffic, since they scorn the goods of this world and deal rather with those of the next . . . I will add still one more word about them. They have been fairly and justly apportioned to the two sexes. He is the ornament of men, she of women, and not only an ornament but also a pattern of virtue.

Again, St. Gregory is effusive in his praise of his mother:

> It is impossible to mention anyone who was more fortunate than my father. I believe that if anyone, from the ends of the earth and from all human stocks, had endeavored to arrange the best possible marriage, a better or more harmonious union than this could not be found. For the best in men and women was so united that their marriage was more a union of virtue than of bodies. While beauty, natural as well as artificial, is wont to be a source of pride and glory to other women, she is one who has ever recognized only one beauty, that of the soul. . . . She rejected paint and other artificial means of adornment befitting women of the stage. She recognized only one true nobility, that of piety, and the knowledge of our origin and final destiny. The only wealth she considered secure was to strip one's self of wealth for God and the poor, and especially for kinsfolk whose fortunes had declined.

As though presenting her as a model for homemakers, St. Gregory tells of her efficiency in the execution of her household duties:

> While some women excel in the management of their households and others in piety—for it is difficult to achieve both—she nevertheless surpassed all in both, because she was pre-eminent in each and because she alone combined the two. She increased the resources of her household by her care and practical foresight according to the standards and norms laid down by Solomon for the valiant woman. She devoted herself to God and divine things as though she were completely removed from household cares. In no wise, however, did she neglect one duty in fulfilling the other; rather, she performed both more effectively by making one support the other.

St. Gregory also mentions that St. Nonna "subdued her flesh by fastings and watchings," cared for widows and orphans, and relieved the misfortunes of the distressed.

Nonna survived her husband by a few months and died in church while participating in the Holy Sacrifice. She is thought to have been of a considerable age when she died in 374. St. Nonna is named in the *Roman Martyrology* and her feast is kept by the Greek monks of Grottaferrata, near Rome.

THIRTY-SIX

BLESSED PAOLA GAMBARA-COSTA

1473–1515

WHEN Paola was only twelve years of age, a marriage was planned for her and a young nobleman, Lodovicantonio Costa. When the child showed reluctance to the plan, the famous Franciscan, Bl. Angelo da Chiavasso, was consulted for his opinion of the matter. In spite of Paola's wishes to postpone the marriage to a later time, Bl. Angelo pronounced that "the Lord had called His servant to the married state." Undoubtedly heartsick at the decision, Paola could do nothing but offer the sacrifice of her life to the will of the Almighty. Having been born in Brescia on March 3, 1473, Paola was married at the age of twelve, with all the pomp and celebration suited to the high rank of both families.

During the early days of her marriage and in the years thereafter, Paola lived a virtuous live—in acute contrast to the laxity of the age in which she lived. Soon after her marriage, the young bride's virtue was demonstrated when she composed the rule which she meant to follow for the rest of her life. This she submitted to Bl. Angelo, her spiritual director, for his approval. The rule stated that she was to rise every morning at dawn to recite morning prayers and the Rosary in the chapel of the castle. Later she was to visit the Franciscan church in the neighborhood and attend Holy Mass. In the afternoon she was to recite the Office of Our Lady, and at bedtime she was to say another Rosary and her night prayers. And her duties to her husband were not overlooked in her rule, since the following clause was included: "I will always obey my husband, and take a kindly view of his failings, and I will do all I can to prevent their coming to the knowledge of anyone."

Three years after her marriage, when Paola was a mere fifteen years old, her eldest son was born. Other children are also known to have joined the family.

Paola's biographers point out her extravagant generosity to the poor, which seems to have awakened her husband's resentment. As long as food was plentiful, her generosity did not annoy him, but in seasons of scarcity beggars swarmed to the castle to reap the benefits of her charity. Biographers point out, however, that in the case of grain, oil and wine, a supernatural multiplication seems to have taken place in proportion to Paola's generosity, so that her household was actually richer for her charities.

Eventually the young wife was confronted with a terrible trial, in the form of her husband's infidelity. Her husband became so bold in his immoral activities that he actually introduced into the castle a young woman of dubious character. She served him as a spy and became the actual mistress of the household. Paola suffered great humiliation from this ordeal and was concerned about the soul of her husband and his immoral friend. When her husband's mistress fell ill, Paola demonstrated her extraordinary charity by devotedly nursing her. Paola was successful in winning the woman's conversion by having her confess her sins to a priest before she died.

Still another trial confronted Paola, when she was accused of having poisoned her rival as an act of revenge. It was noted that the woman's body was found swollen, and the illness had terminated more quickly than would have been expected. But because of Paola's patience, charity, and virtue, she was able to prove her innocence and regain her husband's affection. He returned to the Sacraments and the practice of his faith and allowed his wife to engage in her devotions and works of charity. The rest of Bl. Paola's life is said to have been passed in self-imposed penances and in peaceful wedlock.

Bl. Paola died on January 24, 1515, when she was forty-two years old. After her death she was honored as a saint by all who knew her. She eventually was beatified by Gregory XVI in 1845.

THIRTY-SEVEN

BLESSED PEPIN
OF LANDEN

D. 646

PEPIN of Landen, the Duke of Brabant, had the distinction of being the husband of Blessed Itta (Itte, Iduburga) and the father of Grimoald and two sainted daughters, St. Gertrude of Nivelles and St. Begga.

Considered to have been the wisest statesman of his time, he was mayor of the palace for three monarchs: King Clotaire II, King Dagobert I, and the youthful King, St. Sigebert.

When King Dagobert succumbed to a sinful life, Pepin boldly rebuked him and continued to show his disapproval until the king repented. But when Bishop St. Amandus also attempted to convert Dagobert from his dissolute life, Dagobert banished the Bishop from the realm. Somehow, even though Pepin's disapproval was just as severe and unrelenting as was the Bishop's, Pepin seemed indispensible to the king, and he remained securely at court.

King Dagobert held Pepin in such high regard that he placed his son, St. Sigebert, in Pepin's care when Sigebert was only three years old. When the doting father crowned the child King of Austrasia, Pepin was entrusted with the education and care of the youth. Just before Dagobert died in 638, he demonstrated the trust he placed in Pepin's honesty by appointing Pepin to serve as administrator of the kingdom for his successor, the eight-year-old King Sigebert. A man of lesser worth might have taken advantage of the situation to enhance his own fortune and position, but the trust Dagobert had in Bl. Pepin was well-placed.

While serving in the capacity of administrator of the kingdom, Pepin relied upon the advice of two holy bishops, Arnulph of Metz and Cunibert of Cologne—and though a faithful minister to the King, he placed his foremost duty to the King of kings.

Pepin considered himself the humble servant of the people. He protected Christian communities of the north against the war-like invasions of the Slavs; he worked hard for the spread of the Christian faith, and he appointed the most virtuous and learned men to serve as bishops.

Pepin was described as "a lover of peace, the constant defender of truth and justice, a true friend of all the servants of God, the terror of the wicked, the father of his country, the zealous and humble defender of religion." He was also a wise and virtuous man who cared for young Sigebert as though he were his own son. Under Pepin's guidance, Sigebert became a saint and is regarded as one of the most blessed among the French kings.

Even with all the official duties that fell to him, Pepin did not neglect his family. He and his wife, Bl. Itta, trained their children in virtue and instilled in them a love of all that was holy. The eldest of their three children, St. Begga, married Ansigisilus and became the mother of Pepin of Herstal, who grew up to become founder of the Carolingian dynasty. St.

Gertrude (d. 659) served as the first abbess of the monastery founded by her mother at Nivelles and was regarded as a saint immediately after her death.

Blessed Pepin died in 646 and was buried at Landen, but his body was later translated to the monastery founded by his wife at Nivelles, where it lies in the same tomb as that of St. Itta and close to the altar of his daughter, St. Gertrude of Nivelles.

THIRTY-EIGHT

SAINT PHARAILDIS

D. 740

A VIRTUOUS maiden who had secretly consecrated her
virginity to God, Pharaildis was forced by her parents to marry a wealthy suitor. Having obeyed her parents by
participating in the marriage ceremony, she resolutely determined to keep her vow and steadfastly refused to live with her
new husband in the married state. Rejected and refused mar-
ital privileges, the new husband brutally mistreated his young
wife. We are not told how long the marriage endured, but at
length the husband died, leaving Pharaildis a widow—with
her virginity intact.

Little else is recorded of this saint, except that she died
about the year 740. There were reports of various translations of her relics and numerous miracles worked through
her intercession. She became a very popular saint in Flanders
and is known by different variations of her name: Varelde,
Verylde or Veerle.

In art St. Pharaildis is sometimes pictured with a goose
or loaves of bread. The goose may be connected with the city
of Ghent, or Gand, where the saint was born and where her
relics repose. The bread is connected to a miracle which is said
to have been worked beside her tomb. The miracle involves a

beggar who was praying at the tomb; kneeling close by was a woman who was holding bread in her apron. When the beggar noticed the bread and asked for a piece, the woman hid the loaves and declared that she had nothing to give him. She later discovered that the loaves had been turned into stones.

St. Pharaildis is said to have caused a fountain of fresh water to spring out of the ground at Bruay, near Valenciennes, to relieve the thirst of harvesters. The water of this spring is thought to relieve children's disorders. St. Pharaildis is invoked by mothers who are anxious about the health of their children.

THIRTY-NINE

SAINT PHILIP HOWARD

1557–1595

A DISTINGUISHED group stood around the gold baptismal font in the Chapel Royal at Whitehall, including Mary Tudor and her court; Philip II, the Catholic monarch of Spain who was godfather; and Thomas Howard, the fourth Duke of Norfolk, who was the father of the three-day-old infant, Philip Howard. The baptismal service was conducted by Nicholas Heath, the Chancellor of England and the last Catholic Archbishop of York. The date was July 2, 1557. The infant, who inherited the title of Earl of Surrey, was the future heir to other titles and property: the dukedom of Norfolk, the earldom of Arundel and the baronies of Fitzalan, Clun, Oswaldestry, Maltravers, Mowbray, and Seagrave.

Philip's mother, who had taken seriously ill after his birth, never rallied and died less than two months later. His father, Thomas Howard, a Protestant, remarried soon afterward. Of this marriage, two sons and a daughter were born. After the death of his second wife, Thomas Howard once again married—this time to Elizabeth Dacre, a widow, who brought one son and three daughters with her.

To his extensive properties in Norfolk, Thomas Howard added others through his three marriages and was by far the richest man in England. Anxious to keep the estates in his family, Thomas Howard decided that his own children should marry the Dacre children. By his first two marriages he had three sons and one daughter; the Dacres included three daughters and one son. Such a perfect pairing must have seemed to him a proof of a divine endorsement. Thus it came about that at the age of twelve, Philip Howard, the future saint, was publicly and willingly betrothed to his stepsister Anne.

After the death of his third wife, Thomas Howard, filled with family pride, contemplated marriage with Mary, Queen of Scots, who was then in captivity. His intentions were construed as a plot to dethrone Elizabeth, to assassinate her, and re-establish Catholicism in the realm. Throughout the trial that resulted, Thomas Howard pleaded his innocence, but he inevitably was found guilty of high treason. On September 24, 1571, from his cell in the Tower, he wrote to the fourteen-year-old Philip the following advice:

> Serve and fear God above all things. . . . Love and make much of your wife. . . . Strengthen your young and raw years with good counsel. Make your abode at Cambridge, which is the fittest place for you to promote your learning in. Beware of the court, except it be to do your prince service, and that, as near as you can in the lowest degree, for that place has no certainty.

Thomas Howard was beheaded on June 2, 1572. Because he died a supposed traitor, his son, Philip, was not permitted to succeed to the dukedom of Norfolk. Philip did become the Earl of Arundel and Surrey, though, by virtue of his mother's family.

Philip followed his father's advice and attended Cambridge University, where he excelled in his studies. His memory was exceptional. Once he tested it by memorizing all the house signs on the left side of the street from St. Paul's to Temple Bar. On reaching home, he called a servant and dictated them in order. He then sent another servant to check the list. He had not missed a single sign and all were in the correct order. His powers of recall were such that he could recite perfectly a page of English, Latin, or Italian which he had read through only once.

While at Cambridge, it was noted that "he was tall of stature, yet ever very straight, long-visaged and of comely countenance. . . . His memory was excellent, his wit more than ordinary. He was naturally eloquent and of a ready speech."

During the ceremony in which he received his degree, he professed that the Queen was the Supreme Governor of the Church. About this time he married Anne, who also conformed outwardly to the new religion.

By virtue of his titles, Philip was welcomed at the court of Queen Elizabeth. Dazzled by the new life that now opened up to him, Philip vied with other courtiers to win the special favor of the Queen, who only a few years earlier had signed his father's death warrant. He completely disregarded his father's advice to serve in the "lowest degree," and instead drew ever more extravagantly on his vast fortune in order to cultivate the favor of the Queen.

When Queen Elizabeth dined at Howard House on her return to London, Philip was solidly established in the royal favor. The court Chronicle for these years lists his frequent gifts to Elizabeth and the plays in which he took part for her diversion.

Once again Philip conveniently forgot his father's advice

to "Love and make much of your wife." Instead, his young wife was deeply unhappy and shamelessly neglected, since there was no place for wives in the court of Elizabeth I. Despised and abandoned while Philip squandered both his and her fortunes, Anne was deeply hurt when rumors reached her that Philip was casting doubts on the validity of their marriage. This prompted her to make a desperate appeal to win him back. When her offer of a reconciliation was rejected, she went to live with Philip's grandfather, the Earl of Arundel, who accepted Anne as his own daughter.

In addition to the extended amounts of time Philip stayed at court and the costly gifts he gave to the Queen, Anne had other reasons for leaving her husband. Philip, it seems, was living a dissipated life. One biographer claims that, "There can be little doubt that at this time he was unfaithful to his wife." In a manuscript text now at Arundel, it is recorded that "he patronized corrupted, immodest women with which the court in those times did too much abound."

Upon the death of his maternal grandfather, Henry Fitzalan, the Earl of Arundel, with whom Anne had lived during her husband's time at court, Philip inherited the title and more property. He was then twenty-three years old and had the prestige of being considered the premier earl of England. After the Earl's death, Anne felt homeless and returned to Howard House where Philip, at first, resented her presence. But while he was still frolicking at court, Philip weakened under Anne's gentleness and gradually grew kinder and closer to her.

At this time, Anne was contemplating a complete return to Catholicism. Previously, she had conformed outwardly to the new religion, but maintained a secret love for the Faith of her childhood. In time she was secretly restored to the good graces of the Catholic faith. Philip approved of his wife's brave decision, which he himself was not prepared to make.

Meanwhile the Queen, always quick to notice any cooling of enthusiasm in her courtiers, observed Philip's changing mood. It wounded her vanity to see him giving less attention to her and more to his wife. Philip was then enduring various conflicts. He thought seriously of returning to the Faith after hearing the recently captured St. Edmund Campion (1540–1587) defend the Faith against a group of Protestants. But there was also the certain possibility of his being imprisoned and martyred should his return to the Faith become known.

After Anne gave birth to her first child, a daughter, Philip thought to please the Queen by baptizing the child in the Protestant church and naming her Elizabeth. But sometime in the year 1584, Philip was reconciled to the Catholic faith. There is a tradition that he paced up and down in his torment. His first biographer wrote that after his return to the Faith, Philip "lived in such a manner as he seemed to be changed into another man, having great care and vigilance over all his actions and addicting himself to piety and devotions."

While staying at the Charterhouse in London, Philip "kept a priest by whom he could frequently receive the Holy Sacraments and daily have the comfort to be present at the Holy Sacrifice, whereto with great humility and reverence he himself in person would many times serve."

During the time of his conversion and until the time of his death, Philip was particularly penitent for the way he had treated his faithful and admirable wife during his frivolous time at court. In a letter to St. Robert Southwell he wrote, "I call Our Lord to witness that no sin grieves me anything so much as my offences to that party. He that knows all things knows that which is past is a nail in my conscience and burden the greatest I feel there; my will is to make satisfaction, if my ability were able."

Parliamentary records show that during the winter of 1584, Philip attended regular meetings of the Lords and took his turn at court ceremonies. He knew that he would eventually come under suspicion for the obvious change in the manner of his conduct. Realizing that he and his wife were in danger, Philip consulted the only Jesuit free in England, Fr. William Weston. Philip then decided to leave England. Before he left with his family, Philip wrote a long letter to the Queen, explaining that he had come to realize that if he remained in England, he "must consent either to the certain destruction of his body or the endangering of his soul." He proposed to leave his native country, but "not his loyal affection for her Majesty." Before the letter was delivered, he boarded a ship, but having been betrayed by one of his domestics (some believe that a letter to Cardinal Allen had been intercepted), he was seized at sea and brought back to London, where he was committed to the Tower (1585).

When a charge of treason could not be substantiated, he was arraigned on three other charges: reconciliation with the Catholic Church, attempted flight from the kingdom without the Queen's permission, and correspondence with Cardinal Allen. He was sentenced to a term of imprisonment to be determined at the Queen's pleasure.

Sometime after Philip's imprisonment, Anne gave birth

to their second child, a son, but news of the birth was deliberately kept from Philip as a punishment. When the birth could no longer be concealed, his jailers were instructed to torment him with the false information that it was another daughter. His greatest trial during this time is said to have been his separation from Anne.

Philip had spent eleven years at court; he was to pass ten years in prison. But he was not without the consolations of the Church, since he corresponded frequently with St. Robert Southwell. Also imprisoned was a priest named William Bennett, who secretly celebrated Holy Mass, which was usually served by Philip.

When England was on the alert for the approach of the Spanish Armada, the prisoners considered that many Catholics would be slaughtered after the landing, and they began to pray earnestly for the safety, or at least the salvation, of those who would be killed. Following the defeat of the Spanish Armada, someone falsely reported that Philip had prayed for the defeat of England and for the success of the Spanish invasion. Because of this report, Philip was brought to trial before his peers and was falsely charged with high treason for having prayed for the success of the Spanish invasion, for having harbored priests, and for having corresponded with Mary, Queen of Scots. Philip was convicted of the charges, based on the testimony of false witnesses. On April 14, 1589, he was sentenced to death.

The execution never took place. As the Bishop of Tarrasona wrote,

Tis true he was not executed, but permitted to die a lingering

death under a tedious confinement, being kept a close prisoner for 10 years . . . during which time he gave himself up to
a strict and penitential course of life and to continual prayer
and contemplation, to the great edification of all that knew
him.

During the whole of his imprisonment, Philip was denied
visits from his wife and family members, but he was permitted to correspond with them. He also wrote verses and papers
on religious topics, and spent time in translating a number of
devotional books.

What was surprising during this long and solitary confinement was his cheerfulness. He had great confidence in the
mercy of God and wrote to a friend:

> I assure you, I prepare myself as much as my weakness and
> frailty will permit, and I had rather perform more than come
> short of what I promise, especially wherein my frailty and
> unworthiness and infinite sins may justly make me doubt
> of the performance. But I know God's mercy is above all,
> and I am sure He will never suffer me to be tempted above
> my strength; and upon this I build with all assurances and
> comfort.

During his imprisonment, Philip chipped an inscription
into the wall, above the fireplace in his cell: "The more suffering we endure in this world, the greater our glory in the
next." It was signed "Arundell" and was dated June 22, 1587.
Beneath the name, a later prisoner added the words: "*Gloria
et honore coronasti eum, domine.*"—"With glory and honor
you have crowned him, Lord." (*Ps.* 8:6). On another wall
of his cell Philip carved a small crucifix, about three inches
high. Both the inscription and the crucifix are now protected

behind glass and can be seen in the Beauchamp Tower.

Philip's last prayer was to see his wife, his daughter, and the son who was born after his arrest. This was refused, except on condition of his attendance at a Protestant church. His freedom likewise rested on this condition.

Having entered prison in robust health at the age of twenty-eight, Philip Howard endured ten years of confinement before dying, a gaunt and wasted figure, at the age of thirty-eight on October 19, 1595. Philip was first buried in the same grave in the Tower church that had received the remains of his father.

In his will, Philip left a portion of money to be distributed among "the lame and poor of London within three months of my death." In the event that the Catholic religion would be restored in England, he provided that both Howard House and his house in Norwich should be given to religious communities, and that all the religious lands in his possession should be restored to the Church. He had intended also, in such an event, to build a family chantry and was resolved, in case he outlived his lady, to leave the world and become a monk.

In 1624 Anne transferred his remains to West Horsley in Surrey, and then to a family vault in Arundel.

After Queen Elizabeth's death, Anne was held in high regard by all who knew her. Her days were devoted to prayer, nursing the sick, and rescuing orphans. When she died at the age of seventy-three, she was buried next to the remains of her husband.

In 1874, when the cause of canonization of the English martyrs was first introduced at Westminster, Philip was included with those who had died on the scaffold. With them he was beatified by Pope Pius XI in 1929. In October 1970, with Edmund Campion, Robert Southwell, and thirty-seven others, he was canonized by Pope Paul VI.

A year following his canonization, Philip's remains were brought from the Fitzalan Chapel and were enshrined in Arundel Cathedral. In 1973 the dedication of the cathedral was changed from "Our Lady and St. Philip Neri," to "Our Lady and St. Philip Howard." St. Philip Howard is the patron saint of the diocese of Arundel and Brighton.

When Philip died, his son Thomas was ten years old. He succumbed to the glamour of the court and apostatized, but before his death he returned to the Faith. His son, and Philip Howard's grandson, was Bl. William Howard (Viscount Stafford), who died for the Catholic faith at the time of the Oates Plot. He was the last martyr of the English Reformation.

FORTY

SAINT RICHARD

D. 722

THIS saint was an English prince who belonged to a family of saints. As a result of his marriage to Winna, Richard claimed St. Boniface as his nephew. Also, Richard's three children—sons Willibald and Wunibald, and daughter Walburga—are all honored as saints of the Church.

When Richard's son Willibald was a child and had fallen ill, those who tended him despaired of his recovery. Richard, by his fervent prayers, obtained the child's miraculous restoration to health when he placed Willibald at the foot of a great crucifix which stood in a public place in England.

Taking his two sons with him, Richard started out on a pilgrimage to Rome. He stayed for a time at Rouen and visited most of the holy places along the way, but he did not reach his destination. Richard died suddenly at Lucca, Italy, in 722 and was buried there in the church of San Frediano, where his relics still remain. Following the burial, his two sons continued the pilgrimage and prayed for their father at Roman shrines.

Richard's son Willibald continued on to the Holy Land and settled at Monte Casino while on his way home. The pope, visiting Rome on another occasion, authorized the publication of Willibald's adventures, which is considered to be the first German guide book. When St. Boniface notified Gregory III that he needed help in evangelizing Germany, the pope sent Willibald. In the year 741, Willibald was consecrated the first Bishop of Eichstätt. There he built a monastery, where the strict monastic rule was observed.

Richard's other son, Wunibald, after his ordination, founded in Heidenheim (in the diocese of Eichstätt) a double monastery where men and women, in separate living arrangements, observed the rule of St. Benedict. Wunibald governed the monks, while his sister, Walburga, who had taken the veil in England, ruled as abbess of the nuns.

An unusual situation is observed with respect to the bones of St. Walburga. For four months each year, between two of the saint's feast days, October 12 and February 15, a mysterious oil drips from the bones of the saint. This has taken place for over 1,200 years. Thus far, science had been unable to produce an explanation for the occurrence.

St. Richard is mentioned in the *Roman Martyrology* on February 7.

FORTY-ONE

BLESSED ZDISLAVA BERKA

D. 1252

ORN in Leitmeritz (Litomerice), Czechoslovakia, in the early part of the thirteenth century, Zdislava was pious as a child, and at the age of seven is known to have left home to live in the forest as a solitary. She spent only a short time in her retreat before she was found and returned home.

After some years, in spite of her great reluctance, Zdislava was forced by her family to marry a man who is said to have been noble and wealthy. Zdislava became the mother of four children, but her home life was unhappy due to the disposition of her husband, who treated her brutally. But by exercising extreme patience and gentleness, she was able to obtain a certain freedom in the practice of her devotions and her many works of charity. She made herself at all times the mother of the poor and especially of the fugitives who, during the troubled days of the Tartar invasion, approached her home at Gabal for assistance.

During the time of the invasion, Zdislava helped a sick and fevered mendicant, to whom she gave a bed in her home. When her husband returned and saw the repulsive condition of the religious, he became indignant at her hospitality and was prepared to eject the patient, when suddenly he found in the bed not the poor religious, but a figure of Christ Crucified. Deeply impressed by this miracle, Zdislava's husband relaxed certain restraints he had placed on his wife and permitted her to establish a Dominican priory at St. Lawrence, and to join the Dominican Third Order.

Zdislava is said to have had visions and ecstasies, and during those days of infrequent Communion, she is known to have received the Blessed Sacrament almost daily.

When Zdislava fell terminally ill, she consoled her children and her husband by saying that she hoped to help them more from the Father's Kingdom than she had ever been able to do in this world. She died on January 1, 1252 and was buried in the Dominican Priory of St. Lawrence, which she had founded.

It is recorded that shortly after Zdislava's death, she appeared in glory to her sorrowing husband, who had grown to appreciate the many virtues of his holy wife. This apparition greatly strengthened him in his conversion from a life of worldliness.

The veneration paid to Bl. Zdislava from the time of her death was approved by Pope St. Pius X in 1907.

YOUTH

FORTY-TWO

SAINT AGNES

D. 304 OR 305

THE name Agnes, meaning "chaste" or "pure" in Greek, seems appropriate for one who is regarded among the foremost of the virgin martyrs of the primitive Church. Not only is she one of the most popular Christian saints, but her name is also commemorated in the Canon of the Mass.

Born in the city of Rome, the young saint had a brief life. St. Ambrose (d. 397) claims that Agnes was twelve years old at the time of her death, while St. Augustine (d. 430) states that she was thirteen.

Pope Damasus (d. 384) informs us that immediately after the promulgation of the Imperial Edict against the Christians, Agnes voluntarily declared herself a follower of Christ. Another source maintains that her riches and beauty excited the young noblemen of the first families of Rome, who became rivals for her hand in marriage.

When Agnes refused all of them because of her vow of chastity, one of the young men spitefully reported to the governor that Agnes was a Christian. When a judge could not persuade her to marry nor to renounce her faith, he threatened her with confinement in a house of immorality and death by fire. Agnes calmly listened to his threats and quietly proclaimed her confidence that God would protect her body from defilement. Her only concern was the defense of her modesty, since she was later disrobed before the gaze of a heathen audience. Her flowing hair is said to have sufficiently concealed her nakedness.

St. Ambrose reported in the sixth century what took place when Agnes entered the house of sin:

> When her hair was loosed, God gave such length and thickness to her flowing tresses that they seemed to cover her completely; and when she entered the cell she found an angel of the Lord there waiting for her, who surrounded her with a dazzling light, by reason of the glory of which none might touch or look upon her. The whole room shone like the dazzling sun of midday. As Agnes knelt in prayer, Our Lord appeared and gave her a snow-white robe. The Prefect Symphonianus' son, the prime mover in the prosecution, came with some young companions to offer insult to the maiden; but suddenly falling on his face he was struck dead, and his terrified companions fled, half-dead with pain and terror. At Agnes' prayer the youth was restored to life and converted to Christianity. The people cried out that she was a sorceress and had raised him by magic.

The Prefect was disposed to release her, but feared the people and the Emperor; so he went away and resigned his office to the Deputy-Prefect, Aspasius by name, who confined Agnes to prison.

The prison in which the saint was kept can be visited in the crypt of the Roman church, Sant' Agnese in Agone, located across from the Piazza Navona. In the vaulted chamber of the crypt are frescoes which depict the angels who accompanied and watched over St. Agnes.

St. Ambrose continues:

The Deputy-Prefect, Aspasius, commanded a great fire to be lighted [in the Piazza Navona] before all the people and caused Agnes to be cast into it. Immediately, the flames divided into two, scorching the people on both sides, but leaving the saint untouched. The people ascribed this marvel to witchcraft, and the air was loud with screams and cries of "Away with the witch!" Then Aspasius, impatient at the excitement of the people, bade the executioner plunge a sword into her throat. When Agnes heard the sentence she was transported with joy and went to the place of execution more cheerfully than others go to a wedding.

St. Ambrose tells us in his sermon *De Virginibus* of the year 377 that, "This child was holy beyond her years and courageous beyond human nature. . . . She stood, prayed, and then bent her neck for the stroke . . ."

The saint died in Rome in the year 304 or 305. Burial was in the cemetery, afterwards called by her name, beside the *Via Nomentana.* After the death of Agnes, those who prayed at her grave were constantly harassed and wounded by non-Christians.

Among those who visited the grave was the saint's foster sister, St. Emerentiana, who was still a catechumen and had not yet been baptized. She was, however, baptized—not in water, but in her own blood—when she was stoned to death because of her faith. Her body was laid close to that of St. Agnes, who had died two days earlier.

Over this grave Constantia, the daughter of the Emperor Constantine, erected a basilica, *Sant' Agnes Fuori Le Mura* (St. Agnes Beyond the Walls). Below the main altar of this basilica is found a silver shrine given by Pope Paul V (1605–1621) which contains the relics of St. Agnes and those of her foster sister, St. Emerentiana.

Since the fourth century the saint's feast day has been observed on January 21. On this day each year two white lambs are offered in her basilica during High Mass and are cared for until the time for shearing. Their wool is woven into the pallia given to archbishops throughout the Church as symbolic of the jurisdiction that ultimately derives from the Holy See. A pallium, a band measuring two inches wide and decorated with six purple crosses, is placed over the archbishop's head and worn about his shoulders, falling in the front and back in the shape of a letter Y. The archbishop may wear the pallium only on special occasions, and it is always buried with him. The investiture of the Pope with the pallium at his coronation is the most solemn part of the ceremony and is a symbol older than the wearing of the papal tiara.

Although some claim that the saint was killed by a sword thrust into her throat, others maintain that she was beheaded. Supporting this latter claim is the fact that the *Sancta Sanctorum* at the Lateran is in possession of the head of the saint, which was discovered in 1901 when Pope Leo XIII gave permission for the examination of the treasury after it had been closed for a number of years. According to Dr. Lapponi, an archaeologist, the dentition (arrangement of the teeth) of the skull shows conclusively that the skull belonged to a child of about thirteen years. As the result of other studies, the relic was declared to be authentic. It was further observed that the body was found without a head when the relics of the saint were examined in her church in 1605.

St. Agnes is commonly represented in art with a lamb

and a palm, the lamb being originally suggested by the resemblance of the word *agnus* (lamb) to the name Agnes.

FORTY-THREE

BLESSED ALPAIS

D. 1211

ALPAIS was a peasant girl who was born into lowly circumstances at Cudot in the Diocese of Orleans, France. Because of her family's humble situation, she was obliged to work with her father in the fields until she was stricken by a disease which may have been leprosy. Her biographer, a Cistercian monk of Escharlis who knew her personally, assures us that Bl. Alpais was cured of the disease during a vision of Our Lady. Later, due to the effects of another illness, she lost the use of her limbs and was confined to bed.

It was soon noticed that Bl. Alpais subsisted entirely on the Holy Eucharist. This was confirmed by the archbishop after a commission which he organized had examined and tested the authenticity of her fast. In fact, Bl. Alpais seems to be the earliest mystic of whom it is recorded on reliable evidence that she lived for years on the Blessed Eucharist alone.

Because of Bl. Alpais' Eucharistic fast and her reputation for holiness, the archbishop had a church built next to her home at Cudot so that, by means of a window, the invalid could assist at religious services.

Pilgrims, prelates, and nobles came to Alpais for advice; even Queen Adela, wife of Louis VII of France, visited her three times. In 1180 the Queen made a substantial donation to the canons of the church, "for love of Alpais."

The honor which had been bestowed on Bl. Alpais from the time of her death was approved by Pope Pius IX in 1874.

FORTY-FOUR

BLESSED ANTONIA MESINA

1919–1935

NESTLED in the mountainous interior of Sardinia is the little city of Orgosolo, which became the birthplace of Antonia Mesina on June 21, 1919. Her father, Agostino Mesina, who is described as being handsome, tall, and lean, was a corporal in the cavalry whose assignment was to guard the rural areas around the community of Orgosolo. Antonia's mother, Grazia Raubanu, was noted for her great piety and her appreciation of her daughter Antonia, whom she frequently called "the flower of my life." There were ten children in the family, Antonia being the second-born.

Around the time of her birth, a disease known familiarly as the Spanish fever was claiming the lives of many children. It became the practice during the epidemic for children to be confirmed at an early age. For this reason Antonia was confirmed shortly after her baptism.

During her infancy and early childhood, Antonia was like all children, being lively and playful, as well as obedient and affectionate. When she was old enough to attend school, she was described as being well-liked by both her teachers and the students. Her instructors also stated that Antonia was well-behaved, precise, and studious. In addition to being punctual for class, she loved the duties she was asked to perform, and she exhibited a commendable spirit of sacrifice in bending to the wishes and welfare of her classmates.

Antonia received her First Communion at the age of seven, and at the age of ten she joined an organization for young people known as Catholic Action. She was proud to be a member and encouraged many to join the group, saying that to belong was a beautiful experience and that it "helps one to be good."

It was during Antonia's school years that her mother developed a heart condition. Unable to strain herself or lift anything heavy, Grazia found it necessary to depend almost entirely upon the help of the young Antonia, who was forced to leave school after attending elementary classes for only four years.

Taking over much of the household chores, Antonia helped her mother with the cooking, the care of the children, the cleaning and marketing. The washing of clothes and the carrying of water into the house also fell to her charge; these and her other responsibilities she performed willingly and diligently, as though she were much older. It was also noted that she was always ready to renounce her personal pleasures in favor of the needs of the family.

According to the testimony of family members and those who knew her, Antonia performed all her chores joyfully, and serenely accepted the family's modest economic condition and the hard work and sacrifice this entailed. She was also affectionate and tender with the other children in the family, and she was submissive and obedient to her parents. Her mother was proud to claim that Antonia "never once went against me."

One of Antonia's tasks was the weekly baking of bread. It was her custom to grind the grain, sift it, prepare the dough and gather wood for the baking.

On May 17, 1935, when Antonia was sixteen years old, she asked her friend Annedda Castangia to accompany her into the forest while she gathered wood for the oven. While the two girls were strolling along the path toward the woods, Antonia asked Annedda if she would like to become a member of Catholic Action. When Annedda said that she could not join because of the cost, Antonia encouraged her to join the group by saying that there were no expenses and that there were many spiritual benefits to be gained from the good works they performed and the catechetical instruction they received.

In a deposition, Annedda reported that she could remember details of what next happened as though she had just witnessed them. After gathering a sufficient amount of wood, the girls were preparing to return home when they noticed a teenaged boy along the path. Annedda recognized him as a student from her school, but since he turned onto a different path, the girls thought no more of him. In a few moments Annedda heard Antonia scream desperately for help. The youth had sneaked up behind Antonia, grabbed her by the shoulders and was attempting to force her to the ground. Annedda tells that Antonia broke away twice, but she was caught a third time and knocked down. The would-be rapist then grabbed a rock and struck Antonia repeatedly on the face and head. Mortally wounded, Antonia continued to resist.

Annedda screamed for help and ran to the nearest house to report what was taking place. The captain of the police was hastily summoned and he, together with other citizens, quickly rode into the woods on horseback. There they found the bloody and brutally wounded body of the sixteen-year-old Antonia. Her face was horribly disfigured from the fierce beating and was hardly recognizable as the formerly beautiful face of the virtuous little housekeeper they had always admired. After an autopsy, it was determined that Antonia's body had not been sinfully violated. Like Maria Goretti, Antonia had died a martyr of holy purity.

Antonia's companion identified the assassin; he was captured, tried and condemned to death.

During the Process for her beatification, Antonia's remains were exhumed from the local cemetery. A grand procession of the townspeople, led by the bishop and several priests, accompanied the relics to the Church of the Holy Saviour, where they now recline in a black marble tomb. Both the tomb and the memorial stone that marks the place of martyrdom are frequently visited by Antonia's devotees.

Antonia Mesina was beatified on Sunday, October 4, 1987 by Pope John Paul II. Also beatified during the same ceremony were Blessed Marcel Callo and Blessed Pierina Morosini—all three being twentieth-century lay people and martyrs.

FORTY-FIVE

SAINT ARTHELAIS

D. 570

THERE lived in Constantinople during the reign of the Emperor Justinian a beautiful and virtuous girl named Arthelais, the daughter of the proconsul Lucius and his wife, Anthusa. Many young men proposed marriage, but the emperor, on learning of Arthelais' extraordinary beauty and grace, sent messengers to her father requesting that the girl be turned over to him. Completely shocked by the request, the family decided that the only way to avoid dishonor was to escape from the emperor's jurisdiction. Secret arrangements were made for Arthelais to journey to her uncle, Narses Patricius, in the city of Benevento.

Her father escorted her as far as Buda in Dalmatia, where he left her to complete the journey under the escort of three trusted servants. Hardly had the father left them when they were attacked by robbers. Arthelais was seized while the servants panicked and made their escape. After being held for three days, Arthelais was miraculously released and rejoined her escort. The vengeance of God is said to have fallen upon her captors.

Arthelais and her companions crossed the sea in safety, traveled from Sipontum to Narses, and then to Lucera, and finally arrived at Benevento, where her uncle was expecting her. From the Golden Gate of the city, Arthelais walked barefoot to the Church of Our Lady to offer her thanksgiving for her release and her safe arrival at her destination.

Arthelais then gave herself over to mortification and fasting.

At the age of sixteen Arthelais died as the result of an intense fever and was buried in the Church of St. Luke. Unfortunately, three centuries ago St. Arthelais' church in Benevento was destroyed; it has never been rebuilt. Tragically lost were her relics and artistic representations.

FORTY-SIX

SAINT DOMINIC SAVIO

1842–1857

S T. DON Bosco said of this saint, "In the life of Dominic
Savio you see innate virtue cultivated up to heroism
during his whole life." Dominic was to achieve this heroic
virtue during a lifetime consisting of only fourteen years.

Dominic's exceptional life began on April 2, 1842,
in Castelnuova, Italy; he was the second in a family of ten
children. His parents, Charles and Brigid Savio, were hard-
working peasants who moved to Riva and then to Murialdo,
where Charles found more profitable work as a blacksmith.
Dominic's sanctity can be credited to the early training given
him by his parents, whose faith and devotion served as exam-
ples for their children to imitate.

At the age of five, Dominic was already attending daily
Mass. If he arrived early, before the doors were opened, he
would kneel on the steps in prayer. When he was old enough,
he served Mass almost daily. Although the usual age for
receiving first communion was twelve, the pastor decided that
since Dominic was not only well-prepared but also had an
intense desire for the Sacrament, the boy should be permitted
to communicate at the age of seven.

The day before he received his first Holy Communion,

Dominic begged his mother's and father's pardon for all that he might have done to displease them, and he promised to practice virtue with the help of God.

On the day Dominic was to communicate for the first time, he composed resolutions which were to be his rule for life. He wrote them in a little book and often read them. They were as follows: "I will go to confession and Communion as often as my confessor allows. I will keep holy the feast days. My friends shall be Jesus and Mary. Death—but not sin."

At Murialdo, Dominic finished his primary studies and was then sent to Castelnuova for further study. Since it was necessary for him to walk to school, return for lunch, walk back to school and then return at the end of the day, the walk amounted to eight miles, in all kinds of weather. The boy never complained, and when asked if he was not afraid to walk alone, especially in bad weather, he replied that his guardian angel was with him.

As an example of how Dominic avoided the least influence of sin, we are told that once when he was swimming with a group of boys, they began to make vulgar remarks and to laugh at improper gestures. Dominic immediately left the water, dressed, and went home.

Eventually, his father's work forced the family to move to Mondonio, where Dominic resumed his studies. One day, while the teacher was absent from the room, two boys stuffed snow and trash into the iron stove that was heating the room. When the teacher returned, he became extremely angry. The two guilty boys were so frightened that they falsely accused Dominic of the deed. He remained silent about the matter while he was being scolded before the entire class. When he was later vindicated and asked why he did not defend himself, Dominic replied that Our Lord had also been accused falsely and had remained silent.

Eventually Fr. Cugliero, his teacher, recommended Dominic to St. John Bosco (Don Bosco). The two saints met in 1854. Don Bosco immediately recognized the beauty of the boy's soul, and it was agreed that Dominic should attend Don Bosco's school, the Oratory of St. Francis de Sales. There he became the delight of his teachers, who used his politeness and studious manners as an influence on other boys. Dominic is known to have prevented fights and to have spoken out against tardiness and absence from school.

Once when St. John Bosco preached a sermon on being a saint, Dominic adopted mortifications and penances that were too strict and unsuitable for his age. On learning of these, Don Bosco ordered him to abandon them and instead to observe the following simple suggestions, which can be adopted by all children: to fulfill the duties of his state, that of being a schoolboy; to do good to companions who by nature are displeasing; to forgive those who are vulgar or rude; to consume all food or drink at meals and not to waste anything; to study all subjects at school, even those that are not appealing; to be humble when others are chosen before you for favorite tasks or privileges; never to complain about the weather, but rather to thank God for it; to be bright and cheerful when inclined to be otherwise; and to take advantage of every opportunity to show love for Jesus Christ. Don Bosco concluded by reminding the future saint that "Obedience is your greatest possible sacrifice."

When Don Bosco was displeased with the small number

of boys approaching the Communion railing, Dominic and some of his friends formed the Immaculate Conception Sodality. Their goal was not only to increase the frequency of reception of Holy Communion, but also to promote devotion to the Blessed Sacrament and the Blessed Virgin.

Dominic's life of grace was soon marked by ecstasies before the tabernacle, prophetic dreams, and mystical knowledge of souls in need of Last Rites and of the sick who were in need of prayers. It is told of Dominic that once while at school, he begged permission to return home. There he found his mother close to death during a difficult childbirth. Dominic placed a green scapular on her breast and then returned to school, knowing she would be safely delivered—as indeed she was.

Never in robust health, Dominic became ill and was sent home for a rest; he knew he would never return to the Oratory. At home his condition worsened. He was diagnosed as having inflammation of the lungs, the customary cure being bleeding. This was performed so often that Dominic was soon reduced to a dying state. After reciting prayers for a happy death and receiving Last Rites, Dominic expired on March 9th, 1857, when only fourteen years of age. His last words were, "What a beautiful thing I see."

In 1876 Dominic, accompanied by many holy souls, appeared to Don Bosco in a vision and revealed that he was in heaven. The young saint was canonized in 1954 by Pope Pius XII. He is considered a true model for the youth of our times, since he lived a simple life of virtue—a type of life that can be imitated by youths of all ages.

FORTY-SEVEN

SAINT DYMPHNA

D. 650

DYMPHNA was the only child of a pagan king and a Christian queen, who ruled a section of Ireland in the seventh century. Dymphna bore a striking resemblance to her beautiful mother, an attribute that was to threaten her purity and caused the loss of her life.

After the death of the queen, the inconsolable king, on the verge of mental collapse, consented to the court's entreaties that he distract his thoughts from his beloved wife by marrying a second time. The king's only requirement was that the new wife should resemble his first. Since no one in the country could compare except the daughter, she was suggested as the replacement for her deceased mother. The emotional turmoil of the king allowed this sinful suggestion to seem plausible.

When the illicit marriage was proposed, Dymphna confided the news to her confessor, a pious priest named Gerebern, by whom her mother and other members of the family had been instructed in the Faith. He advised Dymphna to explain to her father the sinful and horrible nature of his proposal, and to pray to God that he would change his mind and ask God for forgiveness for ever having considered such a union. Dymphna obeyed her confessor, but the king was deaf to all her arguments. He appointed a certain day on which the ceremony should take place. Knowing too well the obstinate and vindictive nature of the pagan king, and realizing that it was useless to attempt to change his plans, Gerebern decided that flight was the only means of preserving Dymphna's purity.

Secret plans were made for Gerebern, as well as the court jester and his wife, to accompany Dymphna in her escape from the country. After crossing the sea to the coast of Belgium, they traveled inland and settled twenty-five miles from Antwerp in the village of Gheel, near the shrine dedicated to St. Martin of Tours. With Gerebern instructing them and offering the sacrifice of the Mass, the group led virtuous lives, spending time in devotions and in acts of penance.

The king made a diligent search for his daughter, and followed her as far as Antwerp. From there he sent spies, who discovered the refuge of the fugitives. The clue by which they were traced was their use of strange coins, similar to those which the spies themselves offered in payment.

When the king finally confronted Dymphna, he at first tried to persuade her to return home with him, but he became enraged when he was again unsuccessful in his marriage proposal. When both Dymphna and her confessor attempted to explain the sinfulness of such a marriage, the king indignantly accused the priest of being the cause of Dymphna's disobedience, and ordered his immediate decapitation.

Deprived of the priest's support, Dymphna still remained steadfast. In a fury, her father ordered her execution. When his soldiers hesitated, the king himself severed his daughter's head with his own sword. Dymphna was barely fifteen years of age.

The two bodies were left exposed on the ground for days,

since everyone was afraid to approach them because of the king. The bodies were eventually buried, in a humble manner, by the villagers.

The maiden was soon regarded as a saint, a martyr of purity and a champion over the wiles of the devil, who had brought her father to madness. In due time, those afflicted with lunacy sought her intercession and journeyed to her tomb in pilgrimage.

On account of the growing number of pilgrims, it was decided to give her body and that of her confessor worthier tombs inside the chapel. In digging for the remains, workmen were surprised to find the bodies in two coffins of white stone, of a kind unknown in the neighborhood of Gheel. This gave rise to the legend that the bodies had been reburied by angels after the original interment, since no one could remember their burial in white coffins. When the remains were exhumed, a red stone identifying the maiden was found on the breast of Dymphna.

During the Middle Ages, those who visited Gheel to invoke the saint were encouraged to make a novena of nine days at the shrine, while many afflicted persons participated in seven ceremonies called "penances." Among other practices, they were to attend Mass daily and recite prayers intended to exorcize the demons who were thought to have caused their illnesses. Until the eighteenth century, the same prayers were said in Gheel for all the sick, without distinction between those believed devil-ridden and the mentally ill. During these prayers, the red stone found on the remains of St. Dymphna was hung around the necks of the afflicted.

The relics of the saint are kept in a silver reliquary in a

church that bears her name in Gheel, near Antwerp, Belgium. The church is believed to be situated over the saint's original burial place.

Today St. Dymphna is invoked worldwide for restoration of mental stability, as well as of religious fervor. She is the patroness of those suffering from mental and nervous disorders.

FORTY-EIGHT

SAINT EDWARD, THE BOY KING

D. 979

ST. EDWARD was the son of St. Edgar the Peaceful (d. 975), the sovereign King of all England, and of Edgar's first wife, the beautiful Ethelfleda, who died soon after her son's birth. Edward was baptized by St. Dunstan, the Archbishop of Canterbury, who took a great interest in his upbringing and his advancement in virtue.

When Edward's father died, the whole country is said to have been thrown into a state of confusion since neither of his two surviving sons was old enough to rule. At his father's death, Edward was only thirteen years old. At once the deceased King's second wife, Elfrida, opposed Edward's ascension, even though King Edgar had nominated Edward as his successor. Elfrida wanted the throne for her own son, Ethelred (Aethelred), who was then only seven years old. We might surmise two main reasons for Elfrida's choice: one could have been pride in wanting her own son to succeed to the throne of England; the other was perhaps that Edward had offended many important persons. According to Stenton in his book, *Anglo-Saxon England,* Edward was given to "intolerable violence of speech and behavior . . . his outbursts of rage

217

had alarmed all who knew him, and especially the members of his own household."

It may have been for this reason that a large number of nobles sided with Elfrida in opposing Edward and promoting the election of Ethelred, the younger brother. However, St. Dunstan, the clergy, and most of the nobles rejected the effort and elected Edward in accordance with his father's will.

Under the guidance of St. Dunstan, the young King's temper was brought under control, and he advanced in wisdom and charity while developing into a young man of great promise and virtue.

Historians and biographers all agree that Edward was murdered in a most despicable manner. The details of the crime are given by William of Malmesbury in his eleventh-century biography of Edward. The facts are also mentioned in the early biographies of St. Oswald and St. Dunstan.

St. Edward's untimely death occurred in this manner: On the evening of March 18, 979, after hunting in the forests of Dorsetshire, King Edward was feeling tired; he decided to visit his stepmother, Elfrida, at Corfe Castle, which was nearby. From all appearances, his relationship with Elfrida and his stepbrother Ethelred had grown friendly since his coronation. But in spite of this appearance, William of Malmesbury informs us that since the time of the coronation, Elfrida had developed a hatred of Edward and waited for an opportunity to have him killed. The earliest accounts of the murder state that as Edward approached the castle, Elfrida and several servants went out to meet him with every sign of welcome and respect. Before Edward dismounted, though, the servants surrounded him, seized his hands and stabbed him.

Another report adds other details: As Edward approached, Elfrida was informed that he had ridden well ahead of his company and was alone. Elfrida pretended pleasure at seeing him and ordered a cup of mead to be brought to him at the castle gate. While he was still mounted and drinking from the cup, Elfrida made a sign to one of her servants, who stabbed the young King in the abdomen with a dagger. Edward immediately set spurs to his horse and tried to ride out to meet his attendants, but being weak from the wound and loss of blood, he slipped from the saddle. His leg caught in the stirrup, and he was dragged until he died.

Elfrida had Edward's body thrown into a marsh, thinking to be rid of it altogether. However, a beam of light is said to have caused its discovery. The body was taken up and buried without ceremony in the Church of Our Lady at Wareham. A few years later, Aelfhere of Mercia removed Edward's body to the convent at Shaftesbury Abbey, where miracles soon multiplied. As a result of these reports, Edward was soon regarded as a saint and a martyr. Butler, while admitting that devotion to the saint was widespread and strong, nevertheless states that "Edward's claim to martyrdom is of the slenderest." However, having won the affection of the people, and having been regarded as a defender of the Church and a model of virtue, Edward is recognized by the title of Martyr in all the old English calendars on March 18. He is also regarded as such in the *Roman Martyrology*.

Elfrida reportedly was overwhelmed with remorse for her crime and, in reparation, built the monasteries of Ambresburg and Wherwell. She retired to the monastery at Wherwell and died there after practicing austere penances.

Ethelred was crowned King of England a month after Edward's murder, but he was unable to escape the results of the murder. He reigned in an atmosphere of skepticism which diminished the prestige of the crown. Even though he was too young to have been an accomplice in his brother's murder, the crime had been committed for his sake, and he was never able to escape its memory. Public opinion was still strong against him thirty years after the murder, when Ethelred ordered the general observance of his brother's festival. His reign was troubled with unrest, and it was his fate to be regarded as a weak king. It was never forgotten that, as Stenton puts it, "He had come to power through what his subjects regarded as the worst crime committed among the English peoples since their first coming to Britain."

It is reported that no one was punished for taking part in the murder of the seventeen-year-old king who had reigned for only three and a half years.

FORTY-NINE

SAINT EULALIA
OF MERIDA

D. 304

A HYMN written by Prudentius at the end of the fourth century, along with St. Eulalia's *Acta* of a much later date, give us the particulars of the martyrdom of St. Eulalia, the most celebrated virgin martyr of Spain.

When the edicts of Diocletian were issued, by which it was ordered that all should offer sacrifice to the gods of the empire, Eulalia was a mere twelve years of age. The courage with which the martyrs rejected the edicts and died for the Faith so inspired the young girl that she too wanted to offer her life for her Christian faith. This desire for martyrdom troubled Eulalia's mother to such an extent that she took her daughter into the country. But during the night Eulalia left without telling her mother, arriving at Merida at daybreak.

When Dacian, the judge, entered the court to begin the daily session, Eulalia presented herself before him and declared that he should not attempt to destroy souls by making them renounce the only true God. Dacian was at first amused with the actions of the young girl and attempted to flatter and bribe her into withdrawing her words and observing the edicts. When she firmly renounced this tactic, Dacian then changed his attitude and showed her the instruments of torture, saying, "These you shall escape if you will but touch a little salt and incense with the tip of your finger."

What next transpired startled those in the courtroom. Eulalia at once threw down the image of the false god, trampled on the cake which had been laid for the sacrifice and spat at the judge. The sentence of the girl was quickly pronounced.

Two executioners seized her and took her to a place of torture, where they began to tear her body with iron hooks. As an added punishment for her actions, lighted torches were applied to her wounds. Quite unexpectedly, the fire from the torches caught Eulalia's hair, surrounding her head in flames. Stifled by the smoke and flames, Eulalia died. In his poem, Prudentius tells us that a white dove seemed to come out of her mouth and fly upward. Seeing this, the executioners became so terrified that they fled.

Eulalia's body was entombed by Christians near the place of her martyrdom. Later a church was built over the spot. Of this place Prudentius wrote in his hymn, "Pilgrims come to venerate her bones, and she, near the throne of God, beholds them and protects those that sing hymns to her."

The relics of the twelve-year-old martyr are now found in the Cathedral of Oviedo in a seventeenth-century chapel dedicated to her.

FIFTY

SAINT JUSTUS AND SAINT PASTOR

D. 304

A TOWN formerly called Complutum, now Alcala de Henares, Spain, was the birthplace of these two young saints, who were brothers. Their parents were persons of rank and were Christians who carefully instructed their children in the Christian faith. They were also taught all the things that children of their age generally learn, and thus they attended school every day.

During the Roman occupation of Spain, when the emperor ordered that all Christians should be persecuted, the Roman governor of Spain, Dacian, who hated Christians, went about from town to town seeking those of the Faith and killing those he found. When he arrived at Alcala de Henares, he issued a proclamation that was read in the marketplace, commanding everyone, under pain of death, to offer sacrifice to the gods who were the supposed protectors of the Roman Empire.

The proclamation caused the Christians to be terrified. Justus, who was then seven years old, and Pastor, who was nine, were at school when a messenger approached the teacher to report the news of the governor's proclamation. While some of the students took no notice and continued to work at their lessons, Justus and Pastor listened keenly to the message. They were immediately struck with a supernatural grace and, full of courage, they threw down their books, left school and ran to the place where the governor was interrogating a group of citizens.

The two boys pleaded for his attention and professed that they were Christians. At first the governor avoided them but when they persisted, he marveled that they had come of their own free will to profess a thing that might result in their death. Instead of being mindful of their tender age, Dacian ordered them to be whipped, hoping that this would soon bring them to their senses.

As the two brothers were being led away, they encouraged each other to be unafraid. The officers who heard what they said were amazed that little children could be so willing to suffer for their beliefs.

The children suffered with constancy, and the officers reported the matter to the governor. Dacian was unimpressed by the report or by their youth, but he was concerned about what others might think if he killed them publicly. He then ordered that Justus and Pastor be beheaded secretly in a place where none of the people could see them. They were accordingly led out into a field and were beheaded against a great rock.

The Christians of Alcala de Henares discovered their bodies and buried them at the place where they had died. Later, a chapel was built there, and still later their relics were enshrined under the high altar of the collegiate church at Alcala de Henares.

Although it might seem that the story of the two young martyrs is unworthy of belief, it is said that there can be no question as to the genuineness and antiquity of the cultus of these two saints. St. Paulinus of Nola (d. 431) was so impressed with the supernatural courage of the martyrs that when his own son died at a tender age, he had the child buried close beside the two young saints.

In the breviary of Toledo there is a beautiful and ancient hymn that was written in honor of Sts. Justus and Pastor, preserving all the details of their martyrdom.

FIFTY-ONE

SAINT MAMMAS

D. 275

WHEN the Christian couple, Theodotus and Rufina, was in prison awaiting martyrdom, Rufina gave birth to the future St. Mammas. After the heroic couple's execution, a Christian widow named Amya was favored with a vision of an angel who suggested to her that she should take care of an orphaned infant, who would be found in prison. The good woman found the child Mammas, arranged for legal possession, and raised the boy as her own, instilling in him a great love for the Christian faith. Her efforts were rewarded when Mammas was twelve years old. At that early age he zealously began to make converts to the Faith. Meanwhile Amya died, leaving Mammas heir to certain monies, which he quickly distributed among the poor.

The success of Mammas in winning many converts to the Faith was brought to the attention of Democritus, the governor of the territory. In consideration of Mammas' youth, the governor asked him to sacrifice at the temple of Jove, promising that if he did so, "I will not fail to use my interest with the emperor for your advancement." The saint strenuously resisted. Seeing that he could not weaken Mammas by reasoning, Democritus presented the matter to Emperor

Aurelian, who commanded that Mammas be brought to him. While standing before Aurelian, the saint was tempted by the emperor with these words: "I wish, my son, to employ you at court, but you must therefore abandon the Christian faith. Choose, then, a happy life at my palace or an ignominious death upon the scaffold."

To this St. Mammas replied:

> The choice, O prince, is already made. You propose to me a death which shall render me forever happy, or a short life that must make me eternally miserable. Your gods, which are but deaf and blind statues, can confer no favor upon me. I adore the one only true God, and for Him I am most willing to lay down my life.

This profession of faith so infuriated the emperor that he commanded that the saint's flesh be torn with scourges. Mammas endured this torment with commendable patience. The emperor, who appeared moved by the horrible injuries inflicted upon the tender body of the youth, said in a tone of entreaty, "Mammas, merely say with your mouth that you will sacrifice." But Mammas replied, "It would displease my God were I to deny Him. Continue to torture me as long as it pleases you. . ." The refusal so exasperated Aurelian that he commanded guards to burn the saint with torches. When the guards attempted to apply the fire, they were themselves burned, while the saint remained unhurt.

Aurelian then ordered that Mammas should be thrown into the sea. The hagiography of the saint tells that while he was being led to the water an angel appeared and put the guards to flight. Mammas took refuge on a mountain in the neighborhood of Caesarea and lived in solitude for forty days.

A new governor was appointed in the meantime. When he learned that a Christian, condemned by the emperor, was living on the mountain, he sent a troop of soldiers to seize him. When Mammas was brought before the governor, the latter said to the saint, "You are a rash person, opposing, as you do, the edicts of the Emperor; but torments shall alter you." Mammas was subsequently stretched on the rack, but when he displayed considerable fortitude the governor ordered him to be burned alive. The fire, however, is said to have touched not a hair of his head, but merely to have burned the ropes that bound him. St. Mammas was at last put to the sword. Though still a youth, he nevertheless died a martyr's death, as had his parents.

During the reign of Constantine, a church was built over the tomb of St. Mammas in Caesarea. Although some sources claim that the saint was of noble birth, St. Gregory Nazianzen, relying on other sources, concluded one of his sermons with an allusion to the saint in which he called him "the renowned Mammas, a shepherd and a martyr." St. Basil too mentioned the humble beginnings of the saint in a homily which was intended to illustrate that poverty and humility constitute real glory.

FIFTY-TWO

SAINT MARIA GORETTI

1890–1902

POVERTY dominated the life of the Goretti family from the very beginning. Maria's mother, Assunta, was an orphan who had never learned to read or write. Maria's father, Luigi, after finishing his tour of military service, returned to Corinaldo, Italy, married Assunta and began to farm for a living. The third child of this marriage was our saint, who was born on October 16, 1890. She was baptized the day after her birth and received the names of Maria and Teresa.

Although Luigi worked hard, his small piece of land could not support his growing family. Eventually, when Maria was six years old, the family's situation became so critical that Assunta and Luigi made plans to move from Corinaldo, a place where they had lived in peace and happiness despite their poverty. The Goretti family settled at Colle Gianturco near Rome, where they stayed for two years farming a piece of land with the help of the Cimarelli family. In later years Assunta revealed that their condition there was no better than it had been before, since they were forced most of the time to "live off chestnut flour pudding and maize bread."

After becoming acquainted with the Serenelli family, which consisted of the father, Giovanni, and his son, Alessandro, all three families journeyed to Ferriere di Conca, a place near Nettuno. Here the Serenelli and Goretti families shared a farmhouse called "la Cascina Antica," while the Cimarelli family lodged in a newer house nearby. Arrangements had been made for all three families to work the land of Count Mazzoleni. Unfortunately, malaria was rampant in that area of the countryside and as a result many died. One year and three months after he and his family arrived there, Luigi contracted the disease and succumbed to it. He was only forty-one years old. His widow, who was only thirty-five, was left with six children. The eldest child was twelve years old; the youngest was three months.

After the death of her husband, Assunta was forced to take his place in the fields. Maria, who was then nine and a half years old, willingly and generously assumed the duties of the household and the care of the children. She also assumed the household chores of the Serenellis. She went each day to fetch water from the fountain; she did the washing in the river, and the mending; she frequently went to the Village of Conca to buy household provisions. From time to time she would go to Nettuno to sell eggs and chickens, and with what she got for them she would buy what the family needed, according to the orders of her mother. Normally she walked to Nettuno with the Cimarellis. The journey was scorching in the summer, and the road was often muddy in the winter. While in Nettuno, they would visit the shrine of Our Lady of Graces to confess, attend Holy Mass, and receive Holy Communion.

Assunta revealed that Maria was always obedient because she was of a meek and loving disposition. She also possessed a spirit of mortification, suffering in silence the shortage and sometimes the absence of food. When neighbors gave her sweets, she would always bring them home to share with the other children. We are told that on one occasion, when Maria was doing her customary marketing, a merchant gave her an apple and a sugar cookie, which she slipped into her bag. When the merchant asked why she was saving them, Maria replied that they were for her brothers and sisters.

Maria remained uneducated, her diet was meager, and her responsibilities went far beyond what was considered bearable for one her age. Yet Assunta could not relieve her little family of their squalid and harsh situation, since Giovanni Serenelli kept most of the profits from their hard work.

In spite of the difficulties she had to endure, Maria was a cheerful child who by habit was prompt and obedient, regardless of what was asked of her. In addition to her inherent goodness, Maria was also a beautiful child with light chestnut hair. Her intelligence was also obvious to everyone, as was a certain refinement and a delicacy of personality which seemed out of place in the drabness of the Marshes.

While poor in worldly goods, Maria was nevertheless wealthy in the love of the Catholic faith. It has often been indicated that Maria's sanctity can be attributed to the care with which her mother taught her the basics of the Faith and trained her in the way of virtue. In addition to lessons from her mother, Maria derived great benefit from the sermons of the parish priest at Sunday Mass and from the training she received prior to her first Holy Communion, which was received on June 29, 1901. For this occasion, her clothing and accessories were provided by caring neighbors. According to custom, Maria had already received the Sacrament of

Confirmation at an earlier time.

In later years, Assunta described the prayer-life of the little family:

> At home we would close the day by reciting the holy Rosary, except during summer when sometimes we couldn't manage it as there was so much work to do. Little Maria never missed it; and after her father's death, when we had already gone to bed, she would recite another five Mysteries for the repose of his soul. She did this in addition because she knew that I couldn't have Masses celebrated because I didn't have enough money.

While the Goretti family, headed by the widowed mother, stayed faithful to the practice of virtue, the Serenelli family was very different. In their part of the house the father sought relief from his poverty through alcohol, and both the father and son amused themselves with pornographic magazines. Tragedy was soon to follow, when the youth took the life of young Maria.

About a month before the murder, twenty-year-old Alessandro Serenelli started to give Maria difficult chores to perform and always complained that they were not completed according to his orders. Sometimes Maria was reduced to tears, but she continued to do what was assigned to her. Unknown to Assunta, Alessandro then began to make improper advances to the future saint. Not wanting to burden her mother with another problem, Maria never spoke of it.

On the morning of July 5, 1902, Alessandro ordered Maria to mend one of his shirts. While her mother was busy threshing, Maria sat at the top of the stairs along the outside of the house. Maria placed her little sister, Theresa, on a quilt beside her while she began to do the mending. After a while Alessandro, who had been working with Assunta, excused himself and left for the house. After climbing the stairs he grabbed Maria, pulled her into the kitchen, produced a knife, and demanded that she submit to him. Protesting that it would be a sin against the law of God to do so and that if he did he would go to hell, Maria refused to yield. In a rage, Alessandro stabbed her fourteen times, each in vital areas: the heart, lungs, and intestines.

When little Theresa awoke and began to cry, Assunta sent her son Mariano to quiet the baby and to find Maria. Alessandro's father, who was standing in the shade at the bottom of the stairs, joined Mariano—and together they found Maria, mortally wounded, on the floor of the kitchen. Alessandro was in his room, pretending to be asleep.

At the hospital in Nettuno, surgeons Bartoli, Perotti, and Onesti marveled that Maria was still alive; they operated on the victim for two hours without administering an anaesthetic. Because of her serious condition she was not given the water she asked for, but she did receive Holy Communion, Last Rites, and was made a Child of Mary. For twenty hours Maria lay in excruciating pain, a model of perfect patience and forgiveness. With her virginity preserved, she spent her last hours on earth praying and forgiving Alessandro for what he had done. "Do you forgive your murderer with all your heart?" she was asked. Maria replied, "Yes, for the love of Jesus I forgive him . . . and I want him to be with me in Paradise."

During her final hours of life, Maria often turned her gaze toward an image of Our Lady, and at the prompting of the chaplain she recited ejaculatory prayers. Just before she breathed her last, she called, "Theresa," as though she had suddenly remembered the child she had left on the landing of the stairs. After this she calmly breathed her last. It was three o'clock on the sixth of July, 1902. Maria was eleven years, nine months, and twenty days old.

Maria was buried in the cemetery at Nettuno, but later her remains were removed to the Shrine of Our Lady of Graces, where she had so often prayed and received the Sacraments.

Alessandro was tried for the murder and received a prison sentence of thirty years. For a time he remained unrepentant, but he at last experienced conversion during a vision of Maria, who appeared to him in his prison cell. During this vision a garden appeared before him, while a young girl with dark, golden hair and dressed in white went about gathering lilies. She drew near him with a smile and encouraged him to accept an armful of the flowers. After he accepted them, each lily was transformed into a still, white flame. Maria then disappeared.

Upon his release from prison, the now-repentant Alessandro first sought forgiveness from the saint's mother and then found employment as a gardener in a Capuchin monastery, where he worked until his death. He testified to Maria's sanctity during the Cause of Beatification, as did thirty other witnesses who had known her.

Maria was beatified on April 27, 1947, forty-five years after her death. She was canonized on June 24 during the Holy Year of 1950. Because of the unprecedented crowd attending the ceremony, Pope Pius XII performed the canonization outdoors, the first such ceremony to be held outside St. Peter's Basilica. Present were Maria's brothers and sister and her mother, Assunta, who had the distinction of being the first mother to witness the canonization of her child.

During the time of the beatification and canonization, a wax figure of the saint, which enclosed her bones, was taken to Rome in a glass-sided reliquary; there it was displayed to countless visitors in the Church of Sts. John and Paul. Later the relics were returned to Nettuno.

Among the pilgrims who have visited these relics is Pope John Paul II, who traveled the forty miles from Rome to Nettuno in September of 1979. While in Nettuno, the Holy Father exhorted young people to look upon Maria Goretti as an example of purity to be emulated in this permissive society. The Holy Father also visited a seventy-year-old Franciscan Missionary nun, Sister Theresa, the sister of the saint.

The Cascina Antica, the house where Maria Goretti lived for three years, is often visited by pilgrims. It remains as it was during the saint's lifetime. In the middle of the house on the upper floor is the kitchen where Maria was mortally wounded. A marble plaque indicates the exact place where she was found. Also seen here is a bronze bas-relief, the gift of Pope Pius XII, which vividly recalls the saint's martyrdom. On the exterior of the house the pilgrim can see the steps where Maria was mending Alessandro's shirt shortly before the martyrdom. Pointed out are the bedroom where she had slept in innocence, the threshing-floor where she had played with her brothers and sister, the fountain where she had gone for water, and the exact location along the river where she had washed clothes.

Maria Goretti, a poor, unschooled child who died when not quite twelve years old, is the pride of modern Italy and a model for the youth of the world.

FIFTY-THREE

SAINT PELAGIUS

D. 925

NO DETAILS are given about the parents of Pelagius or about why, when he was a boy, he was in the care of his cousin, Hermoygius, the Bishop of Tuy. What is known is that the boy and his guardian were captured during a battle between the Moors and the Christians of Spain and were taken with other prisoners to Cordoba. Bishop Hermoygius soon grew tired of his confinement, his narrow cell, and heavy chains and was eventually successful in persuading his captors to exchange him for Moorish prisoners who were held in Galicia. Bishop Hermoygius, upon his release, was to arrange for the exchange. By way of hostage, the Bishop left his young cousin, Pelagius, who was then a mere ten years of age.

During the next three years, Pelagius grew into a handsome youth whose high ideals, religious fervor and intelligence merited the respect of his fellow prisoners. He soon came to the attention of Abdur-Rahman, who sent for the boy. Although furious that the Bishop had not fulfilled his part of the bargain by winning the release of the Moorish prisoners, Abdur-Rahman looked kindly upon Pelagius. The boy was offered his liberty, together with horses to ride, fine clothes, money and honor for himself and his parents—but on the condition that he deny his faith. Unimpressed by this offer of worldly goods and a life of privilege, the child of thirteen displayed a maturity and strength of character rarely witnessed in one his age. Pelagius stood firm and is believed to have said,

> All that means nothing to me. A Christian I have been, a Christian I am and a Christian I shall continue to be. These things are transitory and will come to an end, but Christ, whom I serve, has neither beginning nor end; with the Father and the Holy Spirit He is the one true God, who created us from nothing and sustains all things.

When further promises and arguments, and even threats, did not change the youth's mind, he was condemned to death. He was suspended from the gallows, where he was dismembered, his limbs being thrown into the River Guadalquivir.

Pelagius' heroic death in 925 greatly edified the faithful who rescued his remains. His body was honorably buried, but was then taken to Cordoba in 967. Later, the remains were removed to Leon, but when the Moors again threatened in 985, his relics were taken to Oviedo. King Ferdinand of Aragon, in 1023, acknowledged his devotion to St. Pelagius by having the remains placed in a new silver sarcophagus.

The ordeal of the young martyr was sufficiently well-known to attract the attention of the celebrated nun-poetess, Hrotswitha (930–1002), abbess of Gandersheim, who wrote of him in the year 962, thirty-seven years after the boy's death. Her poem praising Pelagius consists of 414 verses.

Many churches throughout Spain were dedicated to the youthful martyr, who is represented in art with pincers, the instruments thought to have been used during his dismemberment.

FIFTY-FOUR

SAINT ROSE OF VITERBO

1235–1252

A S OWNERS of a house and a plot of land, Rose's parents were not destitute, but are said to have lived in humble obscurity in Viterbo, Italy, some forty miles north of Rome.

Rose was born to this hard-working couple about the year 1235 and displayed from babyhood an unusual goodness. At the age of seven she expressed the desire to live alone in a small room of her own so that she might pray undisturbed. When she was eight years old, Rose became seriously ill. On the vigil of the feast of St. John the Baptist, she had a vision or dream of Our Lady, who told her that she was to enter the Third Order of St. Francis and live at home so as to give her neighbors a good example by both word and work. Rose soon recovered her health and was received as a Franciscan tertiary.

The political situation at the time became unsettled when Emperor Frederick II decided to make Rome the civil, as well as the ecclesiastical, capital of the world. With himself as administrator over all, his actions against Pope Gregory IX resulted in the Emperor's excommunication. As a result, Frederick set out to conquer the papal states, and in the year 1240 the Emperor actually occupied Viterbo and the surrounding regions.

Perhaps inspired by a sermon she heard, or by the vindictive words of the enemy, Rose, at the age of twelve, began to courageously defy the enemy by walking up and down the streets while upbraiding the people for submitting to Frederick. She urged them to overthrow the enemy's garrison. Needless to say, the actions of the child drew a great deal of attention, and marvels are said to have accompanied her words.

Eventually, crowds would gather outside her house to get a glimpse of her. As a result, Rose's father became afraid of some unwelcomed retaliation and forbade Rose to leave the house. As enforcement of her father's order, Rose was threatened with a severe beating if she disobeyed. "If Jesus could be beaten for me, I can be beaten for Him. I do what He has told me to do, and I must not disobey Him," Rose replied gently.

After the parish priest expressed his approval of Rose's activities, her father relented and permitted Rose to resume her preaching in public. Aware that crowds were now listening to the twelve-year-old girl, those who sided with the emperor became alarmed and asked that Rose be put to death as a danger to their ambitious endeavor. The officials, however, were fearful of the people if this should be done, and instead ordered that Rose and her parents be banished from the territory. The humble little family then left Viterbo for Soriano.

During their exile, Rose announced in early December the approaching death of Emperor Frederick II. On December 13, in fact, he died in Apulia. Without the main instigator of their endeavors, the enemy retired and peace was restored to Viterbo. The little family happily returned to their home and farmland.

Rose made an attempt to be accepted as a postulant at the convent of St. Mary of the Roses at Viterbo. The abbess, however, refused to accept her. It has been speculated that the sisters did not want an "evangelical preacheress" among them. On hearing the abbess' refusal, Rose said smilingly, "You will not have me now, but perhaps you will be more willing when I am dead."

Rose lived a contemplative life in her parents' house, where she died on March 6, 1252, being only seventeen years old. She was buried in the Church of Santa Maria in Podio—but just as she had predicted, her body was removed six years later to the church of the convent of St. Mary of the Roses. This church was destroyed by fire in 1357, but her incorrupt body was unharmed and is now enshrined in the Monastero Clarisse S. Rosa in Viterbo.

Immediately after Rose's death, Pope Innocent IV ordered an inquiry with a view toward her canonization, but this did not take place until the year 1457.

In 1921, St. Rose's perfectly incorrupt heart was extracted and placed in a reliquary, which is taken in procession through the city every year on the fourth of September, the feast day of the saint. The incorrupt body of the young saint, who died over seven centuries ago, is exposed in a glass-sided casket for the veneration and edification of the faithful.

FIFTY-FIVE

SAINT SIMON OF TRENT

D. 1475

IN THE Office for the Feast of the Holy Innocents we read, "These children cry out their praises to the Lord; by their death they have proclaimed what they could not preach with their infant voices." St. Simon of Trent (Italy) likewise cries out his praises to the Lord, having also died in his innocence at the hands of unbelievers.

Simon of Trent was two and a half years old when he was kidnapped by non-believers who wanted to express their hatred for the Church by killing a Christian child.

One of the kidnappers, a man named Tobias, found Simon playing outside his home with no one guarding him. Simon was enticed away with kindness and was brought to the home of his abductor.

During the early hours of Good Friday, in the year 1475, the child's martyrdom began. His mouth was gagged, and he was held by the arms in the form of a cross. While in this position his tender body was pierced with awls and bodkins in blasphemous mockery of the sufferings of Jesus Christ. After an hour's torture, the child died. The body was kept for a short time before it was thrown into a canal. When the body was recovered, an investigation led to the arrest of suspects.

After confessing their part in the crime, the child's murderers were severely punished.

The remains of little Simon were buried in St. Peter's Church at Trent, where many miracles took place. Simon was awarded the title of saint because of his tender age and the manner of his death.

FIFTY-SIX

SAINT WERNHER

D. 1275

HIS age is not given, but St. Wernher is known to have been a child when he was abducted by non-Christians. Their purpose was to obtain possession of the Blessed Sacrament, or, at least, to use the blood of a Christian child for their magical or cultist rites.

It is believed that Wernher was seized after receiving Holy Communion on Maundy Thursday in the year 1275. He was hung by the heels in the hope that he would disgorge the wafer he had swallowed. When this failed, he was killed. His blood was drained before his body was carelessly thrown into a pit at Bacherach. When the boy's remains were discovered, the murderers were seized and executed for the crime.

Wernher was buried at Trier, where miracles soon occurred at his tomb. His feast was celebrated throughout Germany, but especially in the City of Trier, where the death of the little martyr was remembered with great sadness.

FIFTY-SEVEN

SAINT WILLIAM
OF NORWICH

1132–1144

WILLIAM, the son of Wenstan and Elviva, was born
on Candlemas Day, probably in the year 1132, and
was baptized in Haveringland Church. At the age of eight
he began to learn the trade of a tanner, and in a few years he
was employed in Norwich, England, where furs were in great
demand for clothing and coverlets. William's trade brought
him to the attention of wealthy Jews who lived under the
king's protection near Norwich Castle. This district is now
bounded by White Lion Street and the Haymarket. William
made friends among the Jews, and although such mixed
friendships were not unknown, they were unusual since the
Jews were somewhat distrusted and generally only grudgingly tolerated by the Christians. For reasons not given, it
seems that with the approach of the Lenten season in the year
1144, William's uncle forbade his association with his Jewish
friends. This might have caused apprehension or resentment
within the Jewish community.

For the remaining history of St. William of Norwich
we are indebted to Thomas of Monmouth, who became a
monk of the cathedral priory of Norwich. He investigated the

matter and wrote the details of the murder of William in the second book of his *Vita en Passio.*

Thomas of Monmouth tells us that on Monday in Holy Week in the year 1144, William, who was then twelve years old, was lured away from his mother by someone who offered him employment in the archdeacon's household. A relative of the boy became suspicious of the whole story and followed William and his companion, until he saw them enter the house of a Jew. William was never seen alive again.

The events that next transpired were later revealed by Jewish converts to Christianity and a servant of the house. Their accounts reveal that on Wednesday in Holy Week, after a service in the synagogue, the Jews meant to mock the Crucifixion, in contempt of Christ. They lacerated William's head with thorns, crucified him, and pierced his side. On Holy Saturday, the 25th of March, Aelward Ded witnessed the Jew, Eleazar, and another man carrying a heavy sack to Mousehold, a wooded area near Norwich. When the sack was discovered a few hours later, it revealed William's mutilated body, which bore the clear signs of a violent death.

When word reached the Jewish community that the body had been found, they immediately went to the castle and placed themselves under the protection of the sheriff, who is said to have received a large bribe to guard them. The move was merely an act of prudence, since the boy's mother and relatives soon accused the Jews of the crime.

On Easter Monday, the body was temporarily buried where it lay at Mousehold, and visits were frequently made there by young men and boys who had known the victim. A few days later the priest Godwin Sturt, William's uncle, formally accused the Jews at the Bishop's synod and then had the grave opened; the body was recognized as that of William.

Because of the nature of the wounds and the season of the year in which the Crucifixion had been re-enacted on the boy, the guilt of the Jews seemed confirmed. Since the Jews were then the king's men and under the protection of the sheriff, the bishop, who had also brought charges, had no jurisdiction in the case. A number of bribes were known to have been offered to various individuals to suppress the story or drop the charges in the case. The only result was that the body of the boy martyr was removed on April 24 from Mousehold to the monks' cemetery at the cathedral.

When Aelward Ded, who had discovered the body of the boy in the sack, was on his deathbed five years later, he told what he knew of the crime. As a result, Thomas of Monmouth, the monk chronicler, interviewed a Christian serving-woman who was employed in the house where the crime had been committed. She told how she had peered through a crack in a door and had caught sight of a boy fastened to a post. She had been ordered to bring hot water to her master, presumably to cleanse the body. She afterward found a boy's belt in the room and showed Thomas of Monmouth the marks of the martyrdom that were found in the room. Despite the evidence and the eye-witnesses, no one seems to have been brought to justice for the crime.

Due to the reports of miracles worked through the boy martyr's intercession, William of Turbeville, Bishop of Norwich (1146–1174), on four different occasions had the boy's remains transferred to more honorable places. The last transfer was to the Martyr's Chapel (now the Jesus Chapel) in

Norwich Cathedral. Unfortunately, no trace of St. William's shrine remains, although its site is still known. In 1168, the Bishop erected a chapel in the woods where William's body had been discovered. The site of this chapel can still be visited.

Elias, Prior of the Cathedral (1146–1150), and some of the monks at first were skeptical about the miracles. The doubts of skeptics were overcome, however, when miracles continued to take place, and when several monks had premonitory visions or dreams.

The boy from Haveringland became St. William, martyr, with a feast day on March 24.

INDEX OF SAINTS
THEIR LIVES AND DIFFICULTIES

I T IS our prayer that this Index will be helpful to the lay members of the Church who are trying to live in a truly Christian manner while confronted by the many difficulties and temptations of the world. May these laymen draw courage and determination to endure or overcome their difficulties by examining the lives of the lay saints who also experienced countless trials, but who bravely surmounted them by turning to God and trusting in His holy will. Those who are enduring a particular trial or temptation can discover those saints who experienced a somewhat similar problem by examining the appropriate category of the Index, which is divided thus:

VI   General
        Tertiaries
        Trouble with Family Members
VII   Occupations and Hobbies

An apology might be made to those saints whose faults or sins are featured here. Since these are given with the sole intention of offering an example that might encourage the layman to overcome his difficulties and to advance in virtue, the saints will, undoubtedly, excuse the exposure of their failings.

Through the communion of saints, we can claim these holy people as our blessed friends in heaven. May they pray for us that we will profit by their example so that we, too, may overcome the dangers of this world and merit to join them someday in our heavenly homeland.

I.   MARRIED SAINTS

Married Saints: St. Adalbald of Ostrevant; St. Adelaide; Bl. Albert of Bergamo; Bl. Angela of Foligno; Bl. Anna Maria Taigi; Bl. Castora Gabrielli; St. Catherine of Genoa; St. Clotilde; St. Dorothea of Montau; St. Elizabeth of Portugal; St. Elzear; St. Gengulphus; St. Godelieve; St. Gorgonia; St. Gummarus; St. Hedwig; St. Hedwig, Queen of Poland; Bl. Ida of Boulogne; Bl. Jacoba; Bl. Jeanne Marie de Maille; Bl. Joan of Aza; St. Julitta; St. Leonidas; St. Leopold; Bl. Louis of Thuringia; St. Luchesius; St. Ludmila; St. Macrina the Elder; St. Margaret Clitherow; Bl. Margaret Pole; St. Margaret of Scotland; St. Matilda;

St. Monica; St. Nicholas of Flüe; St. Nonna; Bl. Paola Gambara-Costa; Bl. Pepin of Landen; St. Pharaildis; St. Philip Howard; St. Richard; Bl. Zdislava Berka.

Married Young (19 years and under): St. Adelaide, 16; St. Catherine of Genoa, 16; St. Clotilde, 18; St. Delphina, 15; St. Dorothea of Montau, 17; St. Elizabeth of Portugal, 12; St. Elzear, 15; St. Hedwig, 12; St. Hedwig, Queen of Poland, 13 or 15; Bl. Ida of Boulogne, 17; Bl. Joan of Aza; Bl. Paola Gambara-Costa, 12.

Marriages That Were Happy, But Became Unhappy: Bl. Albert of Bergamo.

Marriages That Were Unhappy, But Became Happy: St. Catherine of Genoa; St. Dorothea of Montau; Bl. Paola Gambara-Costa; St. Philip Howard.

Marriages That Were Difficult or Unhappy: Bl. Anna Maria Taigi; Bl. Castora Gabrielli; St. Gengulphus; St. Godelieve; St. Gummarus; St. Monica; St. Pharaildis; Bl. Zdislava Berka.

MARRIED MEN

Bad-Tempered or Nagging Wife: Bl. Albert of Bergamo; St. Gengulphus; St. Gummarus.

Childless: Bl. Albert of Bergamo.

Couples Separated (amicably or otherwise): St. Gengulphus; St. Gummarus; St. Nicholas of Flüe; St. Philip Howard.

In-Law Problems: St. Adalbald of Ostrevant, wife's family.

Neglected His Wife (before conversion): St. Philip Howard.

Unfaithful Wife, saint who had: St. Gengulphus.

Unfaithful to Their Wives (before conversion): St. Philip Howard.

Vow of Continence (after marriage): St. Elzear.

MARRIED WOMEN

Abused Physically or Verbally: Bl. Castora Gabrielli; St. Godelieve; St. Monica; St. Pharaildis; Bl. Zdislava Berka.

Childless: St. Catherine of Genoa.

Disappointed in Love (loved one but married another): St. Hedwig, Queen of Poland.

Difficult Husband: Bl. Anna Maria Taigi; Bl. Castora Gabrielli; St. Catherine of Genoa; St. Dorothea of Montau; St. Hedwig, Queen of Poland.

Forced to Marry: St. Elzear; St. Hedwig, Queen of Poland; Bl. Paola Gambara-Costa; St. Pharaildis.

Husband Married Previously: St. Adelaide; St. Margaret of Scotland; St. Matilda.

Husband Had Mistress: Bl. Paola Gambara-Costa.

Illegitimate Child (husband's child raised by saint): St. Catherine of Genoa; St. Elizabeth of Portugal.

In-Law Problems: St. Adelaide, daughter-in-law; Bl. Anna Maria Taigi, daughters-in-law; St. Godelieve, mother-in-law; Bl. Jeanne Marie de Maille, husband's family; St. Ludmila, daughter-in-law; St. Monica, mother-in-law.

Jealous Husband: Bl. Anna Maria Taigi; St. Elizabeth, Queen of Portugal; St. Hedwig, Queen of Poland.

Neglected by Husband: St. Catherine of Genoa.

Unfaithful Husband: St. Catherine of Genoa; St. Elizabeth of Portugal; St. Monica; Bl. Paola Gambara-Costa.

Vow of Continence (made during marriage): St. Catherine of
Genoa; St. Hedwig.
Vow of Virginity Made Before Marriage Was Respected after
Marriage: Bl. Jeanne Marie de Maille; St. Pharaildis.

II. WIDOWS AND WIDOWERS

Widows: St. Adelaide; St. Angela of Foligno; Bl. Castora
Gabrielli; St. Catherine of Genoa; St. Clotilde;
St. Dorothea of Montau; St. Elizabeth of Portugal;
St. Hedwig; Bl. Ida of Boulogne; Bl. Jacoba; Bl. Jeanne
Marie de Maille; St. Julitta; St. Ludmila; St. Macrina the
Elder; St. Margaret of Scotland; St. Matilda; St. Monica;
St. Nonna; St. Pharaildis.
Widowers: Bl. Albert of Bergamo.
Saints Who Married Widowers: St. Margaret of Scotland.
Widows Who Raised Children Alone: Bl. Jacoba; Bl. Margaret
Pole.
Widow Who Remarried: St. Adelaide.

III. PARENTING

Mothers of Large Families (5 children or more): St. Adelaide,
6; Bl. Angela of Foligno, several; Bl. Anna Maria Taigi, 7;
St. Clotilde, 5; St. Dorothea of Montau, 9; St. Hedwig,
7; St. Margaret of Scotland, 8; Bl. Margaret Pole, 5;
St. Matilda, 5.
Mothers (1–4 children): Bl. Castora Gabrielli, 1; St. Elizabeth
of Portugal, 2; St. Gorgonia, 3; St. Hedwig, Queen of
Poland, 1; St. Ida of Boulogne, 3; Bl. Jacoba, 2; Bl. Joan
of Aza, 4; St. Julitta, 1; St. Ludmilla, 2; St. Macrina
the Elder, 1; St. Margaret Clitherow, 3; St. Monica, 3;

St. Nonna, 3; Bl. Paola Gambara-Costa; Bl. Zdislava Berka, 4.

Fathers of Large Families (5 children or more): St. Leonidas, 7; St. Leopold, 18; St. Nicolas of Flüe, 10.

Fathers (1–4 children): St. Adalbald of Ostrevant, 4; Bl. Louis of Thuringia, 3; St. Luchesius; Bl. Pepin of Landen, 3; St. Philip Howard, 1; St. Richard, 3.

Adopted Children (saints who adopted): St. Clotilde; Bl. Jeanne Marie de Maille.

Death of Children: Bl. Angela of Foligno, all 7 of her children; Bl. Anna Maria Taigi, 4 children; St. Clotilde, daughter died from husband's abuse; St. Dorothea of Montau, 8 children; St. Hedwig, 3 children died in childhood, 3 as adults; Bl. Jacoba, 2 sons and all her grandchildren; St. Julitta, 1 son; St. Leopold, 7 children; St. Luchesius; St. Margaret of Scotland, 1 son; St. Matilda, 1 son; St. Nonna, 2 children.

Died after Childbirth: St. Hedwig, Queen of Poland.

Difficulty with Parents (saints who had problems with their parents): Bl. Anna Maria Taigi.

Grandmothers Who Raised Grandchildren: St. Clotilde; St. Macrina.

Saints Who Were Stepparents: St. Adelaide; St. Catherine of Genoa; St. Leopold.

Saints Who Had Stepparents: St. Edward, King of England; St. Philip Howard.

Saints Who Had Trouble with Stepparents: St. Edward, King of England.

Young Mothers Who Led a Sinful Life Before Conversion:
Bl. Angela of Foligno.

IV. CHILDHOOD

Born In Prison: St. Mammas.

Died Young: St. Agnes, 12; Bl. Antonia Mesina, 16;
St. Arthelais, 16; St. Dominic Savio, 14; St. Dymphna,
15; St. Edward, King of England, 17; St. Eulalia, 12;
St. Godelieve, 21; St. Justus, 7; St. Mammas; St. Maria
Goretti, 12; St. Pastor, 9; St. Pelagius, 13; St. Rose of
Viterbo, 17; St. Simon of Trent, 2St. Wernher; St. William
of Norwich, 12.

Foster Homes (saints who lived in foster homes): St. Pelagius.

Kidnapped Children: St. Arthelais; St. Simon of Trent;
St. Wernher; St. William of Norwich.

Poor Circumstances (some saints who grew up in poor sur-
roundings): Bl. Alpais; Bl. Anna Maria Taigi; St. Dominic
Savio; St. Dorothea of Montau; St. Maria Goretti;
St. Rose of Viterbo.

Raised by Guardian: Bl. Jeanne de Maille; St. Mammas.

Ran Away from Home: St. Dymphna; St. Eulalia.

Responsibilities When Young: Bl. Anna Maria Taigi;
Bl. Antonia Mesina; St. Edward, King of England;
St. Hedwig, Queen of Poland; St. Maria Goretti.

V. DEATHS OF THE SAINTS

Betrayed By Servant: St. Philip Howard.

Died For The Faith: St. Agnes, d. 304 or 305; St. Eulalia, d. 304; Sts. Julitta and Cyricus, d. 304; Sts. Justus and Pastor, d. 304; St. Leonidas, d. 202; St. Mammas, d. 275; St. Margaret Clitherow, d. 1586; Bl. Margaret Pole, d. 1541; St. Pelagius, d. 925; St. Philip Howard, d. 1595; St. Simon of Trent, d. 1475; St. Wernher, d. 1275; St. William of Norwich, d. 1144.

Died for Purity: St. Agnes; Bl. Antonia Mesina; St. Dymphna; St. Maria Goretti.

Imprisoned for a Time before Martyrdom: St. Agnes; St. Mammas; St. Margaret Clitherow; Bl. Margaret Pole; St. Pelagius; St. Philip Howard.

MURDER

Saints Murdered by In-Laws: St. Adalbald of Ostrevant; St. Ludmila.

Saints Murdered by Relatives: St. Dymphna, father; St. Edward, King of England, stepmother; St. Godelieve, husband.

Murdered by Wife's Lover: St. Gengulphus.

Tortured (some of the saints who were tortured before dying): St. Eulalia of Merida; St. Mammas; St. Pelagius; St. Simon of Trent; St. William of Norwich.

VI.   GENERAL

Abandoned: St. Pelagius.

Accused Wrongfully: St. Dominic Savio; St. Elizabeth, Queen of Portugal; Bl. Margaret Pole; St. Matilda; Bl. Paola Gambara-Costa; St. Philip Howard.

Alcoholism (before conversion): St. Monica showed inclination toward alcoholism.

Cared for Incapacitated Relative: Bl. Antonia Mesina, cared for her mother.

Converts: St. Ludmila; St. Margaret Clitherow.

Criticism (some of the saints who experienced criticism): St. Elzear; Bl. Jeanne Marie de Maille; St. Matilda.

Denied Entrance To Religious Life: St. Rose of Viterbo.

Disliked (some of the saints who were disliked): Bl. Anna Maria Taigi by her neighbors; St. Elzear, father's friend.

Forced To Leave Home (for various reasons): Bl. Jeanne Marie de Maille; St. Macrina the Elder.

Homelessness (some of the saints who experienced homelessness for various lengths of time): Bl. Albert of Bergamo.

Hermits and Solitaries: St. Dorothea of Montau; Bl. Joan of Aza; St. Nicholas of Flüe.

Humiliation (some of the saints who experienced humiliation): St. Gengulphus; Bl. Jeanne Marie de Maille; St. Matilda; St. Monica; Bl. Paola Gambara-Costa; St. Luchesius; St. Philip Howard.

Formally Renounced The Faith And Later Returned: St. Philip Howard.

Mental Condition (saints who may have had psychological problems): Bl. Jeanne Marie de Maille.

Saint Who Endured Another's Mental Disability: St. Dymphna.

Mistakes (some of the saints who made grave or foolish mistakes): St. Ludmila.

Multiplication Of Food: Bl. Paola Gambara-Costa.

Mystics: Bl. Alpais; Bl. Angela of Foligno; Bl. Anna Maria Taigi; St. Catherine of Genoa; St. Dominic Savio; Bl. Jeanne Marie de Maille.

Neglected (some of the saints who experienced this): St. Godelieve.

Nursing the Sick (some of the saints who attended the sick): St. Catherine of Genoa; Bl. Jeanne Marie de Maille; St. Matilda; Bl. Zdislava Berka.

Penitents: Bl. Angela of Foligno; St. Philip Howard.

Political Prisoners: St. Adelaide.

Poor (some of the saints who helped the poor): Bl. Albert of Bergamo; St. Elizabeth of Portugal; St. Gorgonia; St. Hedwig; Bl. Ida of Boulogne; Bl. Jeanne Marie de Maille; Bl. Louis of Thuringia; St. Luchesius; St. Matilda; St. Nonna; Bl. Paola Gambara-Costa; Bl. Zdislava Berka.

Poverty (saints who lived in poverty or were reduced to poverty): Bl. Anna Maria Taigi; Bl. Jeanne Marie de Maille; St. Macrina the Elder.

Rejection (some of the saints who experienced rejection): St. Elizabeth of Portugal; St. Godelieve; Bl. Jeanne Marie de Maille.

Ridicule (some of the saints who experienced ridicule): Bl. Jeanne Marie de Maille.

Sick and Handicapped Saints: Bl. Alpais, invalid; Bl. Anna Maria Taigi, asthma, headaches, rheumatic troubles, hernia, earaches, partial blindness; St. Gorgonia, unusual sickness; Bl. Jeanne Marie de Maille, back trouble.

Slander (some of the saints who experienced slander): St. Elzear.

Temper (saints who endured another's): Bl. Anna Maria
Taigi; Bl. Castora Gabrielli; St. Dorothea of Montau;
Bl. Zdislava Berka.

TERTIARIES

Carmelite: Bl. Josefa Naval Girbes.
Dominican: Bl. Albert of Bergamo; Bl. Zdislava Berka.
Franciscan: Bl. Angela of Foligno; Bl. Castora Gabrielli;
St. Delphina; St. Elizabeth of Portugal; St. Elzear;
Bl. Jacoba; Bl. Jeanne Marie de Maille; St. Luchesius;
St. Rose of Viterbo.
Trinitarian: Bl. Anna Maria Taigi.

TROUBLE WITH FAMILY MEMBERS

Trouble with Mothers: Bl. Anna Maria Taigi.
Trouble with Fathers: Bl. Anna Maria Taigi; St. Dymphna.
Trouble with Sons: Bl. Anna Maria Taigi; St. Clotilde;
St. Elizabeth of Portugal; St. Hedwig; St. Matilda;
St. Monica.
Trouble with a Stepson: St. Adelaide.
Trouble with In-Laws: St. Adelaide, daugher-in-law; Bl. Anna
Maria Taigi, daughters-in-law; St. Godelieve, mother-
in-law; Bl. Jeanne Marie de Maille, husband's family;
St. Ludmila, daughter-in-law; St. Monica, mother-in-law.
Unfair Actions Experienced By Saints (some of the saints
who were deprived of property, money or position):
St. Adelaide; Bl. Albert of Bergamo; Bl. Jeanne Marie
de Maille; St. Macrina the Elder; Bl. Margaret Pole;
St. Matilda; St. Philip Howard.

VII. OCCUPATIONS AND HOBBIES

Administrator: Bl. Pepin of Landen.

Baron: St. Elzear.

Business Woman: St. Margaret Clitherow.

Butcher Shop (worked in): St. Margaret Clitherow.

Councilmen: St. Nicholas of Flüe.

Countesses: Bl. Ida of Boulogne.

Courtier: St. Gummarus.

Crusaders: Bl. Louis of Thuringia.

Duchesses: St. Hedwig; St. Ludmila.

Dukes: Bl. Pepin of Landen.

Empresses: St. Adelaide.

Farmers: Bl. Albert of Bergamo; St. Nicholas of Flüe.

Field Worker: Bl. Alpais.

Governess: Bl. Margaret Pole.

Hospital Workers: St. Catherine of Genoa.

Housewives: Bl. Anna Maria Taigi; St. Dorothea of Montau; St. Gorgonia; St. Margaret Clitherow; St. Nonna.

Judge: St. Nicholas of Flüe.

Knights: St. Gengulphus.

Landgrave: Bl. Louis of Thuringia.

Magistrate: St. Nicholas of Flüe.

Merchants: St. Luchesius.

Philosopher: St. Leonidas.

Pilgrims: Bl. Albert of Bergamo; St. Dorothea of Montau.

Princesses: St. Adelaide; St. Dymphna.

Prisoners (worked with): Bl. Jeanne Marie De Maille; St. Luchesius.

Queens: St. Clotilde; St. Elizabeth of Portugal; St. Hedwig;

St. Margaret of Scotland; St. Matilda.
Scholars: St. Philip Howard.
Shepherdesses: Bl. Joan of Aza.
Soldiers: St. Elzear; St. Leopold; St. Nicholas of Flüe.
Students: St. Dominic Savio; Sts. Justus and Pastor.
Tanner's Assistant. St. William of Norwich.

BIBLIOGRAPHY

Albertson, S.J., Clinton. *Anglo-Saxon Saints and Heroes.* Fordham University Press. Bronx, New York. 1967.

Albin, The Rev. Hugh O. *The Parish Church of St. Dunstan.* Canterbury, Kent, England.

Arnold, Anneliese. *Hospice Built on Hallowed Ground.* Rochester, England. (Paper.)

Aston, Margaret. *The Fifteenth Century.* Harcourt, Brace & World, Inc. London. 1968.

Attwater, Donald. *Saints of the East.* P. J. Kenedy & Sons. New York. 1963.

Aurelius Augustinus, Saint. *St. Augustine's Confessions.* William Heinemann. London. 1931.

Ball, Ann. *Modern Saints—Their Lives and Faces.* TAN Books & Publishers, Inc. Rockford, Illinois. 1983.

Basil the Great, St. *Letters.* Volume II. Fathers of the Church, Inc. New York. 1955.

Beata Angela Da Foligno Lettere Ai Discepoli. Edizioni Chiesa di San Francesco. Foligno, Italy. 1983.

Benedictine Monks of St. Augustine's Abbey, Ramsgate. *The Book of Saints.* Thomas Y. Crowell Company. New York. 1966.

Bessieres, S.J., Albert. *Wife, Mother and Mystic.* TAN Books & Publishers, Inc. Rockford, Illinois. 1952.

Blasucci, Antonio. *S. Francesco Visto Dalla Beata Angela Da Foligno.* Edizioni Chiesa di San Francesco. Foligno, Italy. 1985.

Blunt, Rev. Hugh Francis. *Great Wives and Mothers.* The Devin-Adair Company. New York. 1923.

Brewer, E. Cobham. *A Dictionary of Miracles.* Cassell & Company, Ltd. New York. 1884.

Buehrle. *Saint Maria Goretti.* The Bruce Publishing Company. Milwaukee. 1950.

Butler, Alban; Thurston, S.J., Herbert; Attwater, Donald. *The Lives of the Saints.* 12 Volumes. P. J. Kenedy & Sons. New York. 1934.

Butler, N. V. Pierce. *A Book of British Saints.* The Faith Press, Ltd. London, England. 1957.]

Camm, O.S.B., Dom Bede. *Forgotten Shrines.* MacDonald & Evans. London, England. 1936.

Caraman, S.J., Philip. *Margaret Clitherow.* The Catholic Truth Society. London, England. 1986.

The Catholic Encyclopedia. The Encyclopedia Press, Inc. New York. 1909.

Challoner, D.D., Richard. *Memoirs of Missionary Priests.* Burns, Oates and Washbourne, Ltd. London, England. 1924.

Clarke, James Freeman. *Events and Epochs in Religious History.* James R. Osgood & Co. Boston. 1883.

Colledge, O.S.B., Edmund; Walsh, S.J., James. *Following the Saints.* Good Will Publishers, Inc. Gastonia, North Carolina. 1970.

Conyngham, D. P. *Lives of the Irish Saints and Martyrs.* P. J. Kenedy & Sons. New York. 1870.

Coulton, G. G. *Life in the Middle Ages.* Cambridge University Press. London. 1967.

Cruz, Joan Carroll. *The Incorruptibles.* TAN Books and Publishers, Inc. Rockford, Illinois. 1977.

Cruz. *Relics.* Our Sunday Visitor, Inc. Huntington, Indiana. 1983.

Dahmus. *The Middle Ages.* Doubleday & Co., Inc. Garden City, New York. 1968.

de Grunwald, Constantin. *Saints of Russia.* Hutchinson of London. London, England. 1960.

Delany, Selden P. *Married Saints.* The Newman Press. Westminster, Maryland. 1950.

Delehaye, Hippolyte. *The Legends of the Saints.* Fordham University Press. New York. 1962.

De Liguori, St. Alphonsus. *The Way of Salvation and of Perfection.* Redemptorist Fathers. Brooklyn, New York. 1926.

de Sales, St. Francis. *Introduction to the Devout Life.* Harper & Brothers, Publishers. New York. 1950.

Dickens, A. G. *The English Reformation.* Schocken Books, New York. 1964.

Drane, Augusta Theodosia. *The Life of St. Dominic.* Burns & Oates, Ltd. New York. 1919.

Eglise Fortifiee De Hunawihr. Edite par l'Association des Amis de l'Eglise Historique de Hunawihr. Alsace.

Englebert, Omer. *The Lives of the Saints.* Translated by Christopher and Anne Fremantle. Collier Books. New York. 1964.

Fathers of the Church, St. Basil Ascetical Works. Catholic University of America Press. Washington, D.C. 1962.

Gostling, Frances M. *The Lure of English Cathedrals.* Robert M. McBride & Co. New York. 1926.

Gregory the Great, St. *The Dialogues of S. Gregorie.* The Scholar Press. London, England. 1975.

Hartman, C.SS.R., Rev. Louis F., Editor. *Lives of Saints.* John J. Crawley & Co., Inc. New York. 1962.

Hieronymus, Saint Jerome. *Select Letters of St. Jerome.* William Heinemann, Ltd. London. 1933.

Historia Popular Da Rainha Santa Isabel, Protectora De Coimbra. 5th Edicao Revista e Anotada por Sebastiao Antunes Rodrigues. Grafica de Coimbra. Coimbra, Portugal. 1979.

Iswolsky, Helene. *Christ in Russia.* The Bruce Publishing Co. Milwaukee. 1960.

Jones, Charles W. *Saints' Lives and Chronicles in Early England.* Cornell University Press. Ithaca, New York. 1947.

Lamb, Harold. *The Crusades.* Doubleday & Co., Inc. Garden City, New York. 1931.

Larsson, Raymond E. *Saints at Prayer.* Coward-McCann, Inc. New York. 1942.

Macken, Rev. Thomas F. *The Canonisation of Saints.* M. H. Gill & Son, Ltd. Dublin. 1910.

Mann, Rev. Horace K. *The Lives of the Popes in the Early Middle Ages.* Volume V. Kegan, Paul, Trench, Trubner & Co., Ltd. London. 1925.

Mann. *The Lives of the Popes in the Middle Ages.* Volume XI. Kegan, Paul, Trench, Trubner & Co., Ltd. London. 1925.

The Martyr of Le Ferriere, St. Mary Goretti. Scala Santa, Rome, Italy.

Melis, Mons. Giovanni. *Antonia Mesina Sugli Altari*. Editrice Stamperia Artistica-Sassari. Italy. 1987.

Murphy, S.S.J., Rev. Edward F. *Hand Clasps with the Holy*. Society of the Divine Saviour Publishing Dept. St. Hazianz, Wisconsin. 1941.

Neligan, Rev. William H. *Saintly Characters Recently Presented for Canonization*. P. J. Kenedy & Co. New York. 1859.

Newland, Mary Reed. *The Saints and Our Children*. P. J. Kenedy & Sons. New York. 1958.

O'Connell, Canon J. B., Editor. *The Roman Martyrology*. The Newman Press. Westminster, Maryland. 1962.

Previte-Orton, C. W. *The Shorter Cambridge Medieval History*. Cambridge University Press. Cambridge, Great Britain. 1971.

Riasanovsky, Nicholas V. *A History of Russia*. Oxford University Press. London. 1969.

Sante E Beate Umbre Tra Il XIII Il XIV Secolo. Mostra Iconografica. Edizioni dell'Arquata-Foligno. Foligno, Italy. 1986.

Sharp, Mary. *A Guide to the Churches of Rome*. Chilton Books. New York. 1966.

Stenton, Sir Frank M. *Anglo-Saxon England*. Oxford University Press. London, England. 1943.

Stevenson, J., Editor. *A New Eusebius*. The Macmillan Company. New York. 1957.

Trigg, Joseph Wilson. *Origen*. John Knox Press. Atlanta. 1983.

Undset, Sigrid. *Saga of Saints.* Longmans, Green & Co. New York. 1934.

White, Helen C. Tudor *Book of Saints and Martyrs.* The University of Wisconsin Press. Madison, Wisconsin. 1963.

William of Norwich, (1132–1144.) *Cathedral of Norwich.* (Paper.)

Yonge, Charles Duke. *The Seven Heroines of Christendom.* W. Swan Sonnenschein & Co. London. 1883.